ALONG ROUTE 7:
A JOURNEY THROUGH WESTERN NEW ENGLAND

Stephen G. Donaldson

Schiffer Publishing Ltd®

4880 Lower Valley Road Atglen, Pennsylvania 19310

Dedication

This book was written between November 2008 and January 2009, during the time when Barack Obama was elected the 44th President of the United States of America and subsequently sworn into office. In light of that this book is dedicated to everyone, anywhere, who believes in the true, unadulterated principals of democracy—of absolute equal rights for every individual on the planet; that the greatest good and benefit of our combined efforts should accrue to everyone, and not just to a select few; that we all have a duty to protect and preserve the environment that sustains us; and that the responsibility to ensure these principals starts with each individual assuming an active role in the process and always doing so with pure integrity. It is also dedicated to anyone who holds everyone, including themselves and their family members, to an identical and unwavering set of standards of decency, respect, and common courtesy. From the times of the earliest local Native American tribes to the present day there have been literally hundreds of people whose lives were in some way connected to Route 7 who stood for, and fought for, these same principals.

Cover and book designed by: Bruce Waters
Type set in Zurich BT

ISBN: 978-0-7643-3372-9
Printed in Hong Kong

Cover: Sunrise reveals the stunning beauty of the landscape south of Mt. Philo in Charlotte, Vermont. This is just one of the many world-class vistas that can be viewed from right off of Route 7. On close inspection, Route 7 can be seen flowing from the middle of the right side of the photograph and moving on to the horizon in the center where Snake Mountain, almost 15 miles south, dominates the distant view.

Title page: A clearing storm creates a dramatic setting at sunset in the deep valley that runs from Bennington to Manchester. Little Equinox Mountain provides the imposing backdrop for this scene looking southwest from the shoulder of Route 7 near Manchester."

Schiffer Books are available at special discounts for bulk purchases for sales promotions or premiums. Special editions, including personalized covers, corporate imprints, and excerpts can be created in large quantities for special needs. For more information contact the publisher:

Published by Schiffer Publishing Ltd.
4880 Lower Valley Road
Atglen, PA 19310
Phone: (610) 593-1777; Fax: (610) 593-2002
E-mail: Info@schifferbooks.com

For the largest selection of fine reference books on this and related subjects, please visit our web site at **www.schifferbooks.com**
We are always looking for people to write books on new and related subjects. If you have an idea for a book please contact us at the above address.

This book may be purchased from the publisher.
Include $5.00 for shipping.
Please try your bookstore first.
You may write for a free catalog.

In Europe, Schiffer books are distributed by
Bushwood Books
6 Marksbury Ave.
Kew Gardens
Surrey TW9 4JF England
Phone: 44 (0) 20 8392 8585; Fax: 44 (0) 20 8392 9876
E-mail: info@bushwoodbooks.co.uk
Website: www.bushwoodbooks.co.uk

Once beyond Manchester, Vermont, Route 7 becomes a relatively flat roadway, with only occasional gradual changes of elevation as it emerges from the steep canyon-like valley between Bennington and Manchester and begins to move into the Lake Champlain plateau.

This is one of the few remaining route signs that includes the Ethan Allen Highway plaque. It is located at the merger of Routes 7 and 63 in South Canaan, Connecticut.

Contents

Acknowledgements

I have come to understand that no book project will ever turn out to be as straightforward as one first envisions it to be. This book was, literally and figuratively, a journey and, like any journey I have ever taken, you can only begin with a rough outline and general idea of how to navigate your way to the end. Along the way there will be inevitable twists and turns that don't appear on the map, wrong turns, and tips for intriguing turns you could make just up the road a way. Furthermore, with a book of photography so much is determined by timing, weather, serendipity, and dumb luck. And so, in the end, it usually takes on a form and develops a look that you really had never quite imagined when you started out.

The essential underlying framework for the project is pieced together with several critical elements that include determination, dedication, research, planning, and the generous support and assistance of the many people who inevitably are drawn into the chaos that unfolds.

I have been fortunate to have had literally dozens of people, many of them complete strangers, volunteer their help, knowledge, insight, and hospitality so that I could accomplish this task. At the risk of leaving any one of these many fine people out—and I sincerely apologize to anyone I do leave out—I will try to name them here: Marilyn Douglas, Marie and Richard Hudak, Will Riseley, Ross Liggett, Tony Lake, R. Keith Armstrong, Jeanne Silkworth, Dennis and Judy Mareb, Tim Walsh, Bill Adam, Dan Adam, Ameen-Storm Abo-Hamzy, Leslie Wright, Judith Ellen Johnson, Mary Leitch, Joe and Wanda DiFusco, Matt Sawyer, Pat "Preacher" Hicks, Sydney Hicks, Jennifer Dickemper Hicks, Mary and Harvey Waller, Tyler Deck, Tony DiDomenico, Lenny Meldon, Marge McAvoy, Carol Korzelius, Marylou Chicote, Pamela Fogg, Robert Keren, Jeff Wakefield, Tom McHugh, John Hossley, Dr. DiGrazia, Scott Foster, Armin Palislanovic, Lester Blumenthal, Patty Osmer, John Mitchell, Carol McQuate, and Darlene Brady.

There are many friends who didn't necessarily have anything to do with the making of this book, but whose support and encouragement have always been fuel for my quest to succeed. They are the people who encouraged, inspired, and guided me, and who would always look at me with incredulity when I was down or complaining and say, "yeah, but you're doing what you love to do!" They are: Lisa and David Rubin, Royce Mulholland, Tom Ingersoll, Susan McCaw Ingersoll, Thor and Diane Nickell, Franco Tortoriello, Dan "the Man" Karp, James Randklev, Jeanne Simpson, Ian and Courtney Mitchell, Preacher (again), Christina Fink, Elyse Fink, Susan and Charles Anderson, Sib and Judy Marturana, Sally Heflin and Fatih Yazichi, Jeanne Flynn, Bonnie Cunningham, Susie Hardcastle, Denny and Kim Kinne, Bernie Drew, and many others.

My thanks also to the late Peter Berwind Schiffer, his son Pete, my editor Douglas Congdon-Martin, and everyone at Schiffer Publishing whose excellent work and dedication helped make this book a reality.

To Pop, I wish you could understand and appreciate the things I have worked so hard to accomplish. I'm sorry I didn't get to this point sooner in our lives, at a time when you could have. Ma, sometimes I wonder if I would have ever wanted this if you hadn't given me a copy of *Flavio*—thanks for that original seed of inspiration.

Above all this book is dedicated to Sarah because, were it not for reuniting with her fourteen years ago, I would never have come to live in a place where there would be so much material and opportunity through which my career could begin to flourish. She has always appreciated that I do have a mission and a purpose in my work, and she has always been willing to support that in every conceivable way. She is one of those who understands that I am both crazy and committed enough, to love what I do. Thank you, Sarah, I love you.

No book of mine is complete without some mention of Marquis, the Charcoal Panther, the most nicknamed pet in the history of the planet, whose unconditional love and companionship, and lion's heart, have been priceless assets in my life. Although someday you may no longer be around Bubba, you will NEVER be forgotten.

This view of Monument Mountain from Route 7 in Stockbridge looking across Agawam Lake Wildlife Management Area was taken from the shoulder of the road at sunrise.

The peaks of University of Vermont campus buildings Old Mill and Williams Hall and the steeple of Ira Allen Chapel punctuate the view from the rooftops along Burlington's waterfront. Ira Allen, the brother of Ethan Allen, was one of the founders of the University of Vermont.

Prologue

Although as many as one million people travel on at least some part of Route 7 virtually every day of their lives, few realize that it stretches 308 miles all the way from Long Island Sound to the Canadian Border at the northern edge of Vermont. Many aren't aware that it straddles three states in the process, running in an almost arrow-straight line due north/south, or that it is one of the longest continuous roads in New England that is not an Interstate Highway. Very few know that it was one of the first-ever designated interstate routes in the United States. Furthermore, in 1932 the Hartford Courant noted that it was one of the oldest highways in all of America.[1] For most, Route 7 is just a stretch of road that makes up all or part of their commute to work, or that connects them to the essential goods and services that their daily lives count on.

In a standard road atlas, Route 7, with its very direct path, might appear to be a road with a serious purpose since its designation alternates from "Limited Access Highway," "Interstate," "U.S. Route," and, for long stretches, "Main Through Route." And in many ways it is; much of the regional commerce of western Connecticut, Massachusetts, and Vermont is dependent on Route 7 for the delivery of goods and services, and it is a consistently busy thoroughfare for large truck traffic. But this is a crude and superficial first impression that belies the fact that Route 7 is one of America's great driving roads that should be taken in at a leisurely pace that allows for exploration along the way. It passes through some of the most scenic regions of New England, and what is not seen directly from the road is usually just a few miles off on a less-traveled side road. Indeed, in so many instances Route 7 acts as a gateway to parallel secondary roads or scenic loops that possess some of the most precious offerings along its path. And when you consider that this book can only focus on a fraction of all the stored treasure to be found along Route 7 you can appreciate the richness of the cultural, scenic, historic, and sports-related veins that can be mined here.

However, despite all of its riches and its fine pedigree, Route 7 has remained a modest and understated road, overshadowed and upstaged by roads and highways that garner more recognition, appeal, and cachet in music, literature, and popular media like Route 66, The Blue Ridge Parkway, or the Pacific Coast Highway.

I have traveled the 308-mile length of Route 7 at least 15 times in the last two years and logged in excess of 6,000 miles in order to compile the photographic contents of this book. It is by far the most ambitious and challenging project I have undertaken to date. In the process I have learned a great deal about American history, literature, art, and industry, and I have discovered so much about the geography of western New England of which I was never aware. Yet, as suggested above, every time I look at a map of any part of the Route 7 region I realize that there is even more that I have yet to experience.

Hopefully, then, this book will serve as a virtual journey of discovery for everyone who leafs through it, and it will ignite some flame of curiosity that drives them to explore a new aspect of this great and storied road that they had not previously considered. Of one thing that I am sure; whether you take your journey by way of the book or the road, or, preferably, both, you are bound to enjoy the ride.

Boardman Street, which runs parallel to Route 7 along the opposite (eastern) bank of the Housatonic River from Sheffield to Great Barrington, is one of the easily-accessible side roads that provides some scenic relief from one of the less attractive stretches of Route 7.

Ripton, Vermont, is a little further off the beaten track of Route 7—roughly 3-1/2 miles—but it is well worth the detour since it takes one into the land of Robert Frost and the beautiful wooded back country of Vermont's Green Mountain National Forest. A few miles beyond the Ripton general store, shown here, is Breadloaf, an academic retreat surrounded by stunning high meadows and mountain peaks.

New Milford was first settled in 1707 and its town green still has a turn-of-the-century (20th century that is) appearance from this vantage point. Roger Sherman, an adopted son of New Milford, was one of the authors of the Declaration of Independence. South of New Milford, the Housatonic River diverges from Route 7, flowing in a southeasterly direction toward its estuary on Long Island Sound in Bridgeport, so, depending on which way one is traveling, this is either the first or the last time that the river can be seen along Route 7. North of New Milford the river valley quickly becomes steep and deep, and the road and the river run almost side-by-side all the way to Falls Village.

CANADA

HIGHGATE SPRINGS

SWANTON

ST. ALBANS

ADIRONDACK MTNS

LAKE CHAMPLAIN

NEW YORK

VERMONT

BURLINGTON

SHELBURNE

CHARLOTTE

VERGENNES

MIDDLEBURY

BRANDON

RUTLAND

WALLINGFORD

TACONIC RANGE

MANCHESTER

ARLINGTON

SHAFTSBURY

BENNINGTON

POWNAL

WILLIAMSTOWN

NEW ASHFORD

MASSACHUSETTS

PITTSFIELD

LENOX

STOCKBRIDGE

GREAT BARRINGTON

SHEFFIELD

ASHLEY FALLS

CANAAN

FALLS VILLAGE

WEST CORNWALL

CORNWALL BRIDGE

KENT

BULLS BRIDGE

NEW MILFORD

NEW YORK

CONNECTICUT

BROOKFIELD

DANBURY

WILTON

NORWALK

LONG IS. SOUND

Introduction: The Ethan Allen Highway

The year was 1926, exactly 30 years before President Dwight D. Eisenhower signed into law the Federal-Aid Highway Act of 1956. It was the height of the Roaring Twenties—the age of Gatsby. It was also the height of the Vintage Era in the evolution of the automobile, a period when a significant transition from the production of "open" vehicles to "closed" vehicles transformed the experience of driving and made touring, or long-distance driving, both possible and stylish. With this transition, demand for paved roads exploded and the first nationwide build-out of road systems beyond America's urban centers commenced.

In order to avoid a completely chaotic, dysfunctional, and un-coordinated system of locally and state-funded roads that lacked a national vision, the American Association of State Highway Officials (AASHO), at the urging of state governments and with the blessing of the federal government, established the United States Numbered Highway System. It was decided that north-south running roads would be designated with odd numbers and east-west roads with even numbers. The numbering was started from the farthest eastern point beginning in northern Maine and was worked westward across the country. As a result Route 7 was among the first eight highways to receive a number. This was the ancestor of the more celebrated Eisenhower Interstate Highway System, deemed the "Greatest Public Works Project in History," and it was the essential blueprint for that national road system that was eventually to take shape. The purpose of this earlier system was not just to promote road building in general, but to standardize the road numbering protocols so that there could be continuity in the identity of the primary routes that linked regions of the country together.

Preliminary plans for the makeup of this system were first published in the United States Department of Agriculture's Bureau of Public Roads report dated October 30, 1925 which was approved by the Secretary of Agriculture on November 18, 1925. The initial document included a total of 159 interstate routes spread across the lower 48 contiguous states. In the preliminary census, Route 7, replacing New England Interstate Route 4, was designed to run from Highgate Springs, Vermont, on the Canadian border, to North Canaan, Connecticut, following the current course of alternating sections of Route 7 and Route 7A that pass through Vermont and Massachusetts. In North Canaan, however, the plan was for Route 7 to cut southwest along the former CT 121, joining up with Route 22 in Amenia, New York, and to assume the path of Route 22 all the way south to its terminal point in Mt. Vernon, New York. The master plan was adopted on November 11, 1926 and put into effect the following year.[2]

Thus, for the first several years of its existence, Route 7 was not an all-New England road. However, sometime between 1929 and 1931 a proposal to reroute the road south of North Canaan was approved and the final Connecticut stretch, replacing a patchwork of existing roads, was established so that Route 7 now proceeded from North Canaan almost due south all the way to Norwalk. For the last 78 years, despite a series of failed attempts to convert most of it into a superhighway, the road has essentially stayed intact, although in some relatively short sections it has been widened, merged with Interstates, or rerouted as a bypass to avoid some of the towns and cities along the way. The most significant examples of this involve several stretches of the first 35 miles from Norwalk to New Milford, Connecticut, including where Route 7 merges with I-84 to avoid Danbury, and the adjoining Brookfield bypass; the Lenox bypass in central Berkshire County, Massachusetts; and the roughly 25-mile stretch of divided highway from Bennington to Dorset in southern Vermont that bypasses Manchester.

At about the same time that the new route to Norwalk was established, the last major portion of roadway on Route 7, a 40-mile section running from the Massachusetts-Vermont border north to Manchester, was completed.[3] On September 22, 1930, The *Hartford Courant* ran a three-paragraph article about the dedication ceremony held in Manchester, Vermont, the previous day to commemorate the achievement and to christen the stretch of road from Williamstown, Massachusetts, to Montreal, Canada, the Fort Ethan Allen Highway.[4]

It didn't take long for people all along the route, and throughout the northeast United States, to realize what a gem had been created. Newspaper travel sections and other publications began to write about Route 7 as a premier touring route for driving enthusiasts and it was often cited as one of the most picturesque roads in America. It was also touted as America's most direct route to Quebec, Canada. By 1933 the Connecticut legislature went on something of a road-naming binge and in the wave of enthusiasm Connecticut House Representative W.E. Templeton of Kent, who was the sitting chairman of the Roads, Bridges and Rivers Committee, proposed that Route 7 should become Ethan Allen Highway No. 7 in honor of one of the state's most revered native sons.[5] On August 12, 1932 The *Hartford Courant* reported that the legislation had passed and that the Connecticut portion of Route 7 had officially been named Ethan Allen Highway.[6]

Opposite page
The views from the top of the Equinox Skyline Drive above the Village of Manchester are truly breathtaking. This unique dead-end toll road actually begins in Sunderland off Historic 7A and rises 3,248 feet in 5.2 miles. From this vantage point, accessed from the trails at Equinox Mountain's 3,853 ft. peak, one can see the deep valley through which Route 7 travels. In the far right, framed by the branches of a pine tree, you can see Old Manchester center and the Equinox Resort, and, on the other side of the pine tree, the interchange on the new Route 7 bypass is visible in the area flooded with sunlight.

Fortunately anyone who travels along Route 7 will find that the vast majority of the landscape and its scenic beauty has also remained intact, and the history that unfolded along its path has been meticulously memorialized. Perhaps more than any other single road in the country, Route 7 preserves and embodies so much of the industrial, cultural, academic, political, military, and social history of the United States. Some of Americas most famous writers, sculptors, illustrators, painters, business tycoons, educators, statesmen, entertainers, and musicians have, in one way or another, left their imprint somewhere along Route 7. The list is long and impressive and includes, to name just a small sampling, Robert Frost, Daniel Chester French (sculptor of the Lincoln Memorial), the famous opera singer Marian Anderson, Pearl S. Buck, Norman Rockwell, Herman Melville, Dorothy Canfield Fisher, James A. Farrell, members of the Choate, Lincoln, Vanderbilt, and Morgan families, even contemporary icons like James Taylor, and, of course, Ethan Allen.

The stone marker in Belcher Square, Great Barrington, marks the spot where General Knox passed through town en route to Cambridge to deliver armaments to George Washington's army.

Commemorative plaque in Falls River, Connecticut.

The sign text reads:

PEARL S. BUCK
June 26, 1892 – March 6, 1973

Mother, wife, writer, humanitarian, and civil rights activist, Pearl Buck was the first American woman to receive the Pulitzer and Nobel prizes for literature. A visionary, she worked to cross political and cultural barriers to further understanding among all peoples of the world. Her own perspective was fostered by a life lived equally in China and America and by extensive world travels. She established Welcome House, the first adoption agency specializing in multi-racial adoptions, and the Pearl S. Buck Foundation to aid thousands of children fathered by American servicemen overseas. In 1950 she purchased property in Winhall, VT, and in 1969 moved to Danby, finding an American town she loved, helped restore, and where she died in 1973.

VERMONT DIVISION FOR HISTORIC PRESERVATION - 2000

One of the ubiquitous historic marker signs in Vermont.

13

Allen was not just a favorite native son of Connecticut, he was a true American hero and an icon of the struggle for independence. He was born in 1738 in Litchfield, Connecticut, the seat of Litchfield County. The county occupies nearly one thousand square miles in the northwest corner of Connecticut. Route 7 travels roughly 45 miles through the western end of Litchfield County, following the course of the Housatonic River most of the way.

A series of events in Allen's life would inextricably link him to Route 7. Soon after his birth his family moved to Cornwall, a village just a few miles east of the Housatonic River. As a boy Allen would travel the wagon and coach trails that predated Route 7 by over two hundred years to deliver his father's corn to a nearby gristmill.[7] According to some accounts Allen also worked on the original trail that would become Route 7, felling trees and widening it to accommodate large wagons.[8] In his late twenties Allen and his wife moved to Sheffield, Massachusetts, and lived there for several years. But it was in 1775, at the age of 37, that Allen, as the leader of the Green Mountain Boys militia group, made history for himself and Route 7 by leading his soldiers on a march up the Route 7 corridor through northern Connecticut, Massachusetts, and southern Vermont en route to Fort Ticonderoga, where they seized control from British forces in one of the seminal events of the lead up to the American Revolution.

Not long after the siege of Fort Ticonderoga, Allen was captured by the British and held as a prisoner in England for most of the ensuing three years. After his release Allen returned to America and spent the rest of his life as an activist in the affairs of the new colonial government. He was one of the pioneering settlers of Burlington, Vermont, and built his final home on a large tract of land just about two miles north of what is today the city's downtown area.[9]

It is not surprising, then, that there was such consensus of opinion over proposals to name Route 7 the Ethan Allen Highway in both Connecticut and Vermont and that it carries that name to this day. Much like Ethan Allen, Route 7 is one of those roads that is rarely boring or monotonous; in fact it seems to constantly beckon the traveler to take in the generous helpings of Americana that are offered up just about every few miles or so.

The modest homestead north of Burlington, Vermont, where Ethan Allen spent the final years of his life.

The Congregational Church on the Green in Litchfield, the birth place of Ethan Allen.

History Made & Revealed Along Route 7

Route 7 is truly one of America's great corridors of history and culture, and just as with the story of Ethan Allen, so much of what the region of western New England has to offer is directly tied to the road. Along its path visitors can discover the roots of our colonial development, the first phases of our emergence as an industrial powerhouse, and the early rumblings of the Revolutionary War. They can picnic at the summit of mountains that inspired some of our most classic and enduring novels, visit battlefields where our independence was forged, and stand in the place where baseball traces it origins.

The large stone tablet on the lawn of Great Barrington's Town Hall commemorates the first incidence of armed resistance against British control of the colonies.

The Beckley furnace, which operated along the Blackberry River in Canaan, Connecticut, was a vital source of iron for the manufacture of armaments used in the Revolutionary War.

Opposite page
The Colonel John Ashley House in present day Ashley Falls, Massachusetts, represents the origins of both the United States Declaration of Independence and the Civil Rights Movement.

Long before there was an official Route 7, isolated Native American tribes like the Peaquanock, the Weantinock, and the Schaghticoke—who still maintain a 400-acre reservation near Bulls Bridge, Connecticut—lived along the Housatonic River and began carving out the north-south trails on its banks. These trails became the horse paths and coach routes that linked the many isolated pioneer settlements of the early-mid 18th century and eventually provided one of the many pathways to freedom on the Underground Railroad for African slaves. There are numerous homes along Route 7 from Connecticut to Vermont that served as safe houses on the road to freedom and have either been preserved as museums or posted with historic markers. And, in many ways, long before Martin Luther King was even born, the earliest essential foundations of the Civil Rights Movement were being laid through the accomplishments and struggles of people like Mum Bett and W.E.B. DuBois, whose lives are commemorated along Route 7.

Most research about pre-colonial times in the territory of western New England—the Route 7 corridor—indicates that there were very few organized permanent communities set up by the Native American populations who dominated the surrounding regions. Most Native American settlements in the corridor were located along the shores of Long Island Sound and up-river along the Five Mile, Norwalk, Saugatuck, and Housatonic Rivers as far as present-day New Milford and its environs. The Pequot War of 1637 left most of the territory between Kent, Connecticut, and Rutland, Vermont, in a disputed status, so settlement was sparse and, in many cases, only temporary. Also, it seems clear that the much larger river valleys of the Connecticut to the east, and the Hudson to the west were of far more importance to the Iroquois and Algonquin Nations that controlled most of the northeast. Indeed just one tribe, the Stockbridge Mohegans, was known to control almost all of what is now Berkshire County when European settlers first arrived there. In 1722 their leader, Chief Konkapot, sold their vast holdings to the British pioneers. Northern Vermont between the Green Mountains and Lake Champlain was just as sparsely populated, and some research points to the probability that many of the settlements in this area were only seasonal. Of course, most of what we know about Native American history in the region must be based on archeology, research, and a degree of speculation since there is no written record to work from.

History and modern art collide in a graffiti-style mural dedicated to the life and achievements of civil-rights activist W.E.B. DuBois. DuBois was born and raised in Great Barrington and the mural can be seen on a building wall that faces the main municipal parking area directly behind the commercial buildings that line Main Street/Route 7. The mural was created in 2003 by members of the Railroad Street Youth Project.

So, as is the case in most parts of the U.S., the history that is preserved, commemorated, and celebrated along Route 7 pertains almost entirely to the last 300-350 years, beginning with the pioneering days of colonial settlement of the Americas. As I have suggested above, there is a prodigious and broad cache of history that was created along Route 7 and much of it had far-reaching effects on the rest of the country.

The late 1700s were, of course, dominated by the struggle for independence from the British Crown and in this time western New England became a breeding ground for hard-core revolutionaries like Ethan Allen. In 1773, The Sheffield Declaration, which would serve as the blueprint for the Declaration of Independence, was drafted by a group of men led by Colonel John Ashley. A year later, the first known armed uprising against British rule took place at the courthouse in Great Barrington where Town Hall stands today. The critical battles of Bennington and Hubbardton occurred in the vicinity of modern-day Route 7, and, after Ethan Allen and the Green Mountain Boys seized Fort Ticonderoga, General Knox led his troops through the Berkshires to deliver captured artillery guns to George Washington in Cambridge, Massachusetts, where he employed them to help drive the British out of Boston.

The re-enactment of the Battle of Bennington in North Hoosick, New York, 2007.

Monument Mountain Reservation is one of the sights along Route 7 that straddles the gap between Native American and post-Colonial history. A young Mahican Indian woman, whose love for her cousin was forbidden, jumped to her death from a spot now named Squaw Peak. A pyramid of rocks below marks the spot when she perished. More than 100 years later William Cullen Bryant, while residing in Great Barrington between 1815 & 1825, wrote his poem "Monument Mountain" which celebrates the majesty of the mountain and laments the tragedy of her death. With its commanding 360-degree views of the surrounding central Berkshire landscape, Monument Mountain provides some of the best and most popular hiking trails in Berkshire County.

The blast furnaces in places like Kent and North Canaan, Connecticut, led the early growth of the country's iron industry which in turn fueled the build-out of the railroads and eventually facilitated the drive to the vast western frontiers of the continent.

The Civil War even reached far north to the town of St. Albans, Vermont, where the terrifying St. Albans raid took place on October 19, 1864.

The vigorous expansion and prosperity of the 1800s, culminating in the "Gilded Age," also left its lasting impression on the region. The first industrial age in America brought sea-faring commerce to places like Norwalk, Connecticut, and created thriving mill and mining towns like New Milford, Housatonic, and Bennington. Fueled by this prosperity, the cultural, political and industrial elite from Boston, New York, and other eastern seaboard cities were drawn to the scenic rural beauty of Litchfield County, Berkshire County, and central and northern Vermont, where they built ostentatious mansions that they modestly called summer cottages. Some of these have remained private residences. Many have survived as museums, tourist attractions, and special events venues, or as exclusive hotels, inns, and resorts.

In 1886, William Stanley, Jr., the famous industrial inventor who mastered the nuances of alternating current, made Great Barrington, Massachusetts, the first town in America with electric street lights.

At the turn of the century, and well into the 1900s, much of the wealth that was being generated throughout the country was plowed into public and private projects to build symbols of America's ascendancy on the world scene. Highly sought-after Massachusetts and Vermont marble was quarried in the Route 7 corridor for such iconic symbols of American industry and government as the Lincoln Memorial, the Thomas Jefferson Memorial, The U.S. Supreme Court Building, the Boston Customs House, New York City Hall, Grant's Tomb, and the Empire State Building.

In 1916, Norman Rockwell began his wildly prolific career as an illustrator, painter, and, ultimately, social historian when he sold his first cover illustration to the *Saturday Evening Post.* Although it wasn't until 1953, at the age of 59, that Rockwell took up residence in Stockbridge, Massachusetts, this is the place with which he is most widely associated. The wholesomeness of his subject matter and the often playful manner in which he committed it to paper or canvas have resonated with Americans for generations, and his works will almost undoubtedly always be considered some of the most iconic and expressive American art ever produced.

Finally, in 2004, in a bizarre twist, citizens of Pittsfield, Massachusetts, learned that they lived, in all likelihood, in a city that could make a legitimate claim to being the birthplace of an institution that is part of the bedrock of modern American society—baseball. The news broke at a time when the city was embroiled in marathon multi-year standoff between a group of investors who wanted to build a new municipal baseball stadium and an equally determined group, spearheaded by former New York Yankee pitcher, and author of *Ball Four,* Jim Bouton, who wanted to embark on a significant restoration project for the existing, and profoundly historic, Wahconah Park. While engaged in a research project, baseball historian Jim Thorn discovered the existence of a town ordinance drafted in Pittsfield in 1791 that forbade baseball, and other sports, from being played in the vicinity of the New Meeting House, making it the oldest known document in the country to mention organized baseball. Further investigation ensued and the actual document was found in the archives of the Berkshire Athenaeum in Pittsfield. When the authenticity of the document was eventually verified, the citizens of Pittsfield knew that organized baseball had been played there for almost 50 years before the date when citizens of Cooperstown, New York, believed the game was invented within their town limits.[10]

This represents just a meager sampling of the rich historic, social, and cultural treasure that can be discovered along Route 7. It would literally take a book of encyclopedic proportions to cover everything that could be written about the people, places, and events that have impacted this region. And it is all the more impressive when you consider that the 308-mile stretch of Route 7 occupies just a small sliver in the top right corner of a map of the United States.

The west side of N. Main Street (Route 7) in St. Albans, Vermont, has a row of attractive red brick commercial buildings that are typical of so many of the town centers along Route 7. The buildings overlook Taylor Park and support a variety of shops, boutiques, and cafes.

Wooden covered bridges are ubiquitous along the entire length of Route 7. Driving north from Norwalk the covered bridge in West Cornwall is one of the first, and possibly the hardest to miss, that the traveler will encounter. They are symbols of the expansion of small town society throughout New England in the 18th and 19th centuries, and of the mobility that people enjoyed in the era of the horse-drawn carriage. The West Cornwall Bridge is 172 feet long and was built in 1864.

Edith Wharton visited the Berkshires and fell in love with the area, then proceeded to design her "summer mansion," The Mount, and its classic formal gardens. Wharton was 40 years old when she bought the property in 1902 and she had already smashed conventional barriers by becoming America's first widely published female novelist. The Mount gained national exposure in April, 2006, when First Lady Laura Bush fulfilled a long-standing desire to visit Wharton's masterpiece.

The Gilded Age also left its print in northern Vermont where, in the late-1880s, Dr. William Stuart Webb and his wife, Lila Vanderbilt, created the enormous enterprise that became known as Shelburne Farms. Their principal lake front house had 25 bedrooms and indoor plumbing. Additionally, to support a horse breeding business, Webb had this enormous horse barn built.

Each year the Colonial Carriage & Driving Society, based at the Orleton Farm in Stockbridge, Massachusetts, hosts a number of events in the central Berkshires featuring the opulent horse-drawn carriages and nostalgic sleighs that invoke the Gilded Age. In this image, Robert LaBrie of Townshend, Vermont, drives an Albany Cutter sleigh pulled by his friesian Gurbe, while participating in the annual Winter Classic Sleigh Rally.

For about three years the struggle to preserve the historic Wahconah Park in Pittsfield, Massachusetts, made almost weekly headlines. The choice between saving the park, with which some locals had a love/hate relationship, and losing its triple-A franchise tore the city in two. In the end the new proposed ballpark was voted down and Wahconah held its ground.

First rays of sunshine penetrate the morning fog hovering over Robbins Swamp Wildlife Management Area in Canaan, Connecticut, just off the Route 7 roadway.

Ultimately, if you have ever questioned whether it would be worth taking the time to visit this part of the country and travel along its principal roadway, I would ask that you consider the following:

In 1773 the Sheffield Declaration was drafted by a group of men led by Colonel John Ashley. Much of the philosophical and legal discussion about the validity of the claims and demands of the Declaration was conducted in the presence of Mum Bett, a slave woman owned by John Ashley. In 1776 the Declaration of Independence, inspired by the Sheffield Declaration, was drawn up in Philadelphia by a group of men that included Roger Sherman of New Milford, Connecticut. In 1781, Mum Bett, inspired by the words of her master and his cohorts that she had heard years before and emboldened by the success of the American Revolution, went into the town of Sheffield one day and asked for the assistance of a local lawyer in suing for her freedom based on the principals of freedom and equality expressed in the new Constitution. She won and changed her name to Elizabeth Freeman. The case was tried in Great Barrington, Massachusetts. In February, 1868, W.E.B. DuBois was born in Great Barrington. He was the great-grandson of Elizabeth "Mum Bett" Freeman. W.E.B. DuBois went on to become one of the most tireless and respected activists for the civil rights of African-Americans. He was instrumental in the formation of the NAACP in 1909.[11] In many respects he was a man ahead of his time. He was also a great inspiration to Dr. Martin Luther King. In August, 1963, Dr. King stood beneath the statue of Abraham Lincoln in Washington, D.C., and declared to the world the he had a dream. In 1964, he confided that a significant part of that dream was that within 40 years a black man would become president of the United States of America. On November 4th, 2008, Barack Obama was elected President.

It can, then, be argued that it all began in a parlor in the home of Colonel John Ashley, located in Ashley Falls, Massachusetts, just 100 yards off of Route 7A.

Route 7 Today

It should already be clear that it doesn't matter where you begin your journey along Route 7, or which direction you head in, or if you travel the whole length or just a portion of it, or whether you happen to live somewhere on or near it. Whatever the case, you are bound to experience and see things that will enrich your life along the way. Route 7 is a continuous chain of intimate state parks, storied educational institutions, esoteric world-renowned museums, well-preserved 18th century village squares, excellent restaurants, steepled colonial churches, covered bridges, world-class entertainment, meandering waterways, epic scenery, ever-rising mountain ranges, and challenging trails for bikers, runners, hikers, skiers, boarders, bird watchers, fishermen, leaf peepers, and picnickers alike. Every year people alight onto the Route 7 corridor by bus, train, plane, boat, ferry, car, motorcycle, and bicycle, and some even simply walk onto it as they step off the Appalachian Trail. In fact, anyone who has hiked the entire length of the Appalachian Trail has spent at least several days on and around Route 7.

The entire area is a four-season tourist haven that draws people from all over the world. It is also a region of vibrant, stable communities where many people choose to relocate, and that few desire to leave once they have put down roots there. It lacks any single large metropolitan city, but it is close enough to both Boston and New York City that this isn't such a big deal for most.

When you begin to take advantage of these resources it becomes easy to see the reasons why. As I have traveled to shoot the photography for this book, I have kept track of an informal inventory of a sampling of the variety of attractions that can be appreciated over the entire length of Route 7. Supplementing what I already listed above, it reads like this: five small cities; thirty-two towns and villages; the summer home of the Boston Symphony Orchestra; one large natural lake that was almost granted Great Lakes status; one large man-made lake and at least thirteen other small lakes; three mountain ranges; at least twelve wildlife sanctuaries; two Maritime Aquariums; five completely restored historic theatres; twenty covered bridges; two principal rivers; countless smaller rivers, streams and waterfalls; eighteen major museums; dozens of smaller local historical society museums and at least twenty other historic properties; six colleges and universities; five annual international film festivals and four world-class summer theatre festivals; one historic baseball park; one NASCAR racetrack; twenty golf courses; five Connecticut and two Vermont vineyards; two Revolutionary War battlefields; ten ski resorts; and literally hundreds of fine hotels, inns, resorts, bed & breakfasts, and places to dine, drink, or just get a much-anticipated ice cream. And I'm sure there's plenty more where all of that came from.

Lights from the first annual Tri-State Fair in Pownal, Vermont, reflect off the lake at the former Green Mountain Greyhound Race Track in August 2007.

The Mahaiwe Theatre in Great Barrington, Massachusetts, underwent a massive, $9-million restoration that was completed in 2006. The 100-plus year old theatre was once a thriving vaudeville playhouse, but suffered decades of decay before being resurrected. The building has since been placed on the National Register of Historic Places.

On the actual tarmac, Route 7 is a road with many aliases. As it passes through the villages, towns and small cities along its path it assumes such local names as Van Buren Road, Norwalk-Danbury Road, Danbury Road, Sugar Hollow Road, State Road, Federal Road, Kent Road, River Road, So. Canaan Road, Ashley Falls Road, Main Street, South Street, North Street, Court Street, Lake Champlain Byway, N. Pleasant Street, Shelburne Road, S. Willard Street, Riverside Avenue, and River Street. In order to facilitate its modified route around Danbury it melds with I-84 for several miles and then becomes known as the 43rd Infantry Division Memorial Highway over a four-mile stretch to Brookfield. There are also three sections of the original road that are now marked 7A which run parallel to the newer sections that make up the principal route. Finally, there are two curious short sections between Wallingford and Rutland marked 7B that snake around the main road and link the villages of Pierces Corner and North Clarendon to the highway section of Route 7 that passes through this area.

Of course, beyond all of the history, culture, entertainment, academia, sports, and all of the things that a traveler can stop and do or see along the way, there is one constant, enduring quality of Route 7 that makes it the great driving road that it is, its scenery. As you drive up or down Route 7, and explore the many side roads that network around it, you will constantly enjoy the view from your mobile front row seat. It is a gift that keeps on giving. And while it may be frustrating at times to have to obey the 40, 45, and 50 mph speed limits, and crawl through crowded town centers, you will ultimately be grateful that these inconveniences allowed you to have more time to enjoy the views.

There is one other unusual facet that is worthy of mention here, since it is expressed by much of the local population throughout the year. In a sense, Route 7 is a contemporary sports Mason-Dixon line for the northeastern United States separating Red Sox Nation from Yankee Country and Mets Territory; Patriot Land from The Land of the Giants and The Jets; The Hub of Hockey from the The Garden of the Rangers; and the Boston Celtics' Gah-den from Madison Square Garden, the home of the Knicks. And while the line of Route 7 establishes an clear geographic boundary in this corner of the American sports universe, the territory that spans 20 miles either side of the road is a quintessential grey area for the entire 308-mile span. The mix of sports allegiances along Route 7 is like brackish water in a large river estuary. Neighbors, co-workers, and even family members are often at odds on any given game day in any season.

A crowd displays its split allegiances on Memorial Day in Sheffield, Massachusetts.

course of Route 7 is so eminently appealing. And just as often I tried to photograph things, people, and places I saw that gave character to the journey. There are some photographs taken in winter so that all four seasons have at least some coverage, but the vast majority were taken in spring, summer, and fall since this is when the landscape can be easily explored and most deeply appreciated and enjoyed. In the course of driving the road everyone will get their chance to add their own interpretation to this body of work and fill in whatever gaps or omissions they find.

In the course of their journey everyone will see different things, and people will often see the same things in different ways. This book is sort of like a highlight reel of still images from all of the travel I have done up and down Route 7 from my base in Great Barrington. The following chapters are arranged geographically from south to north by state (which, coincidentally, also allows it to flow alphabetically state by state). The intended effect of this is to provide the reader with a sense of what they might encounter if they traveled the whole length of Route 7 in a single shot, and, ideally, it will be a lasting memento of the journey they had. There is, of course, a lot of iconic subject matter in the photography. However, just as often, the photographs are not of the principal landmarks, but rather of the commonly overlooked aspects and nuances of a given place. I intentionally did not take photographs of every tourist spot because I did not want this to simply be a book of postcards. As often as possible I attempted to find scenic points right on the side of the road to show how much of the actual

While enjoying the Summer Festival and Street Fair in Kent, Connecticut, I was drawn to this display of colorfully decorated umbrellas arranged against the side of a shop. Although it didn't necessarily speak to any particular place I wondered if anyone else who was there that day might have also noticed what I saw and would enjoy seeing this image if they were ever to leaf through this book. It is a sort of message in a bottle.

Connecticut

Norwalk to Danbury

Route 7 emerges from the eastern reaches of New York City-based urban sprawl along the shores of Long Island Sound in Norwalk, Connecticut. From here commuter rail lines, a major interstate freeway, and the Merritt Parkway channel the masses like pulsing arteries into the heart of Gotham every work day.

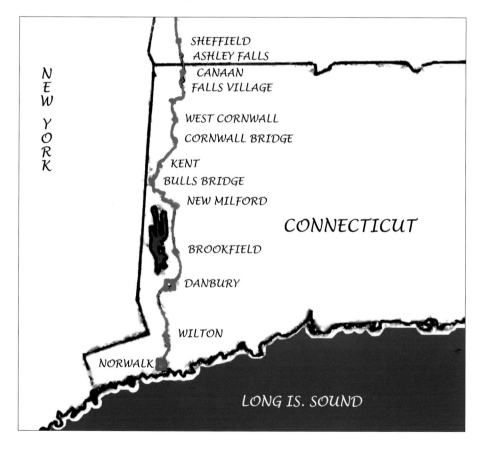

N E W   Y O R K

SHEFFIELD
ASHLEY FALLS
CANAAN
FALLS VILLAGE

WEST CORNWALL
CORNWALL BRIDGE

KENT
BULLS BRIDGE
NEW MILFORD

CONNECTICUT

BROOKFIELD

DANBURY

WILTON

NORWALK

LONG IS. SOUND

MetroNorth tracks on the bridge over the intersection of Washington Street and Main Street in Norwalk's Historic SoNo.

Opposite page
The Maritime Aquarium At Norwalk is the anchor of the city's revitalization project that gave birth to the moniker Historic SoNo.

Norwalk is a demographically diverse city of about 85,000 people, which makes it the largest city located on Route 7. According to town records the area that encompasses modern-day Norwalk was purchased by Roger Ludlow in 1640 when he offered a meager assortment of everyday items like mirrors, knives, scissors, coats, and no money to Chief Mahackamo to "purchase" the territory.

As a seaport Norwalk has a rich history tied to shipping, tourism, and oyster farming. By the late 1800s Norwalk had been nicknamed "Oyster Town," and the largest fleet of steam-powered oyster boats in the world operated from its harbor. In the late 1970s the historic downtown area of Norwalk was granted a stay of execution by the administration of the recently-elected Mayor Bill Collins. After years of decline and decay, the district, filled with classic turn-of-the-century three-and-four storey commercial buildings, had been slated for demolition.

Their efforts culminated in a downtown revitalization and historic preservation plan that became known as Historic SoNo (taking the first two letters of South and Norwalk) which is now anchored by the waterfront Maritime Aquarium At Norwalk and its state-of-the-art IMAX Theatre. The project eventually restored commerce and nightlife, and with it tourism, to the downtown area. The restored vitality is evident in the filled marinas, the river traffic, and the waterfront communities where the real estate has always been considered desirable.

One final little known nugget of information about Norwalk is that it is home to Knipschildt Chocolatier, maker of the world's most expensive chocolate truffle.

The famous mural of the sailing freighter *Alice S. Wentworth* greets visitors to Norwalk.

Historic SoNo in Norwalk.

Historic SoNo in Norwalk.

The Maritime Aquarium At Norwalk.

South Norwalk Boat Club.

The Norwalk River.

Norwalk Harbor viewed from Shorefront Park.

Rowayton, with its placid harbor on Five Mile River, is located in the southwest corner of greater Norwalk. The town also traces it origin to the 1641 land deals between Native Americans and British settlers that gave birth to the Norwalk communities. Its historical development parallels that of Norwalk, albeit on a more modest scale, but the village is probably best known as the birthplace of the business computer due to the creation of the Remington Rand 409 computer in 1951 by engineers working on the estate of James Rand, chairman of the Remington Rand Corporation.

Wilson Cove, between Rowayton and Norwalk.

Rowayton Harbor.

Mill buildings facing the Maritime Aquarium At Norwalk.

From Norwalk's historic district along Washington Street, you pass under the hulking railroad bridge and turn right onto North Main to make the link-up with Route 7 proper and head north out of the city. This is bedroom-community country, and the first 20 miles of the road from Norwalk to Danbury follow a narrow, winding course through hilly country densely packed with some of New York's tony extended suburbs. From a scenic standpoint, the road is mostly featureless, with small businesses and strip malls dominating the tight landscape. To the east and west wooded residential roads meander through the gentle sloping hills of the surrounding towns of Wilton, Weston, Ridgefield, and Redding. One charming attraction just off the east side of the road, about 8 miles north of Norwalk is the historic diminutive town square of Cannondale, a village within Wilton. The vital element of Cannondale is the commuter train station which dispenses a substantial crowd to Stamford and New York City from the surrounding neighborhoods every day. Joe Montgomery commuted to his job on Wall Street from here for several years before quitting to start his bicycle manufacturing company which he named after the station.

There is an inviting coffee shop in the south end of the station building. A late-nineteenth century one-room schoolhouse that has been converted to a restaurant, a specialty grocer called Penny 'Ha' Penny that sells all things British, and an antiques store are arranged in a neat rectangular cluster on the eastern side of the train tracks.

Just over 3-1/2 miles north of Cannondale Village, Route 7 intersects Route 102. The roughly 4-mile detour west along Route 102 takes you through manicured rolling residential countryside en route to the center of Ridgefield where you will find the venerable Aldrich Museum of Contemporary Art and a pristine, quintessentially New England town center. Taking Route 35 northeast out of the town center will get you back to Route 7 about five miles north of the Route 102 intersection. In the process you will have avoided an essentially sterile stretch of Route 7.

Converted one-room school house in Cannondale Village.

The Café au Lait coffee shop at Cannondale Station.

Three of the four national flags of the United Kingdom that hang alongside the Union Jack over the entrance of the specialty grocer Penny 'Ha' Penny can be seen in the photograph. When I saw this, I tried to remember the last time I had seen the Welsh flag displayed in this country and I couldn't think of a single instance. Since I have a great affinity for Wales and the Welsh people, the image of the aligned flags stuck in my mind and this has always been my favorite photograph from Cannondale.

Beyond Cannondale the road maintains its narrow, twisting and predominantly commercial character for the next twelve miles on its approach to Danbury. Over the last several miles, just before the road rises to enter the south side of Danbury and passes the airport, you drive through the Wooster Mountain State Park named after local hero General David Wooster who was killed in the Revolutionary War.

Sometimes there are very personal and whimsical reasons for taking a picture. When I passed by this nursery and landscape ornament business tucked into the steep hillside right on the side of the road in Wilton I immediately thought of Monopoly. I quickly spun back around and took a few shots of the outdoor displays.

This large ornamental clock at the Marvin Gardens nursery probably catches most people's attention as they drive by.

Danbury is a proud, prosperous, and ethnically diverse small city of approximately 80,000 inhabitants. Although there has been settlement in Danbury since 1685, it is, technically, a relatively young city, having been incorporated on April 19, 1889. A large percentage of the original settlers migrated up to the area from Norwalk. Thankfully, in 1687, the original settlement's name was changed from Swampfield to Danbury.[12] The new name was derived from a village in Essex, England.[13]

Civil War monument at the intersection of West Street and Main Street, Danbury, Connecticut

Over the first 170 years of Danbury's existence the city grew slowly, but the population exploded after 1850 due to a manufacturing innovation that transformed Danbury's principal industry. Even to the present time, Danbury is known as Hat City (it was also called "Hat City of the World" at one point) by virtue of the dominant hat manufacturing industry that thrived here for over 150 years. In the early 1800s there were dozens of independent hat shops in central Danbury making hats for domestic sale and for export. However, around 1850, a new machine was introduced that automated the process and spurred the construction of large-scale mills along the Still River ushering in an era of mass production that soon drove the city's annual output to as many as 5 million hats.[14]

The pleasant tree-lined Main Street area, covering a half-dozen blocks, is occupied by a number of beautiful and unique early 20th century buildings including the former Fairfield County Court House, the Greek-revival Savings Bank of Danbury Building, the Library, the Union Savings Bank Building, and the Danbury National Bank Building, which was built from brownstone shipped in from Chicopee, Massachusetts.

The railroads came to Danbury in 1852 and were also an important engine of growth for the city. Freight lines brought efficient supply channels and connected Danbury to distant markets, while the introduction of the Danbury branch of the MetroNorth commuter lines in 1971 finally linked Danbury to New York City for passenger service. The importance of the railroads is celebrated at the Danbury Railway Museum, which operates out of the restored 1903 Danbury Station. One of its most valued possessions is the only operating locomotive turntable in Connecticut. This is one of the wonderful esoteric museums in the region and it is well worth a visit.

It is also interesting to note that Danbury is home to Western Connecticut State University. Charles Ives, one of Americas first classical composers, is a native son of Danbury, and the world famous opera singer Marian Anderson spent the last fifty years of her life in Danbury. Anderson's fame was cemented in 1939 when she gave a concert on the steps of the Lincoln Memorial after having been denied the opportunity to sing in Constitution Hall by the Daughters of the American Revolution because she was black. She is equally well known for being the person who broke the color barrier at the Metropolitan Opera House in New York and for her performance at the Inauguration of John F. Kennedy.[15]

The Seal of Danbury

The Union Savings Bank Building, Danbury.

The former Library, Danbury.

Entrance to the restored station house at the Danbury Railway Museum.

Detail on the exterior of a vintage New York, New Haven, and Hartford line commuter train car.

Conductor of Thomas the Train at the Danbury Railway Museum.

Display of vintage rail yard signal lanterns.

Interior of a commuter rail car display at the Danbury Railway Museum.

Danbury to Bulls Bridge

The most prominent feature of the landscape of north Danbury, and beyond, is Candlewood Lake, the largest lake in Connecticut. The lake is man-made and was created in the 1920s, when a powerful group of lawyers and businessmen bought up large tracts of land and commenced on a plan to flood the Rocky River basin in order to create a source of hydroelectric power. The plant was the first pumped-storage hydroelectric facility built in the United States.[16] It is still in operation and Route 7 passes the power station, and its massive penstock pipes, about a mile north of the New Milford bridge.

Candlewood Lake has a number of parks scattered along its winding shoreline and is a popular destination for boaters and fishing enthusiasts from all over the region.

With its water drawn down and most of the watercraft in some form of dry dock, Candlewood Lake yields to the long winter and takes on the look of a foreboding desolate tundra. However, even in the middle of winter, it hasn't completely lost its utility—note the small hockey rink that has been cleared out just beyond the dock.

Tyler Deck, Tony DiDomenico, and Lenny Meldon drilled fifteen holes through the eight-inch thick ice to spend a day fishing in the middle of the lake. Their catch of one trout and three small perch hadn't been much to brag about, but it was still early.

After disengaging from I-84 northeast of Danbury, Route 7 becomes the 43rd Infantry Division Memorial Highway (or Brookfield bypass) and then continues to run north about 1/2-mile off the eastern side of Candlewood Lake, providing access to dozens of roads that lead up to the lake's mostly residential shoreline. Just east of Brookfield, you can hook up with the western half of the Connecticut wine trail. DiGrazia Winery is a little more than a mile off the road near Obtuse Hill. There are five Connecticut vineyards that are located short distances off of Route 7 on secondary roads: McLaughlin, DiGrazia, White Silo, Hopkins, and Land of Nod.

The next town north of Brookfield is New Milford and it is from this point on that Route 7 abruptly crosses over from the congested and mostly commercial immediate surroundings of its first thirty-plus miles into a idyllic New England landscape. Route 7 joins up with the Housatonic River in New Milford and they remain almost side-by-side from there all the way into Massachusetts.

The DiGrazia Winery in Brookfield, Connecticut produces several varietal wines, but its blueberry wine "Big Blue" has won several prestigious awards and is their flagship product.

New Milford, measuring over 62 square miles, ranks as the largest town in Connecticut by land area. From the time of its first settlement in 1707, New Milford grew up like a number of the towns and cities south of it. Historians agree that relations between Native Americans of the area and the early settlers were harmonious and mutually beneficial.

In the 1800s, many of New Milford's businesses served the textile industry, including Danbury's flourishing hat making juggernaut. Tobacco was also important to the town's growth and, in the later 1800s, the Housatonic Rail Road invested in commercial and industrial development in the town. One notable historic date is March 2, 1949, when New Milford became the first town in the U.S. to have automatic streetlights that were engineered to go on at dusk.

The town center of New Milford is actually located across the Housatonic River from Route 7 and is accessed by the bridge at the intersection of Route 202. The primary commercial streets of the downtown area are Railroad Street, Bank Street, and Main Street. With its rows of three-story red brick commercial buildings, art deco movie theatre, and cast iron street lights festooned with American flags, this shopping district harkens back to another time in history.

But the true hidden gem of New Milford is Lover's Leap State Park, located about a mile-and-a-half south of the town center. The park straddles the Housatonic River gorge where limestone cliffs rise up 100 feet from the river's surface. At the mouth of the gorge is the ornate Falls Bridge, built by the Berlin Iron Bridge Company in 1895. It is one of only four lenticular iron bridges that are still standing in Connecticut.

Interestingly, just above the northern tip of Candlewood Lake and just outside of New Milford, about 1/2-mile off of Route 7, up Route 37, is a small river named Naromiyocknowhusunkatankshunk—no kidding; it's on a map printed by Hagstrom![17]

The bridge over the Housatonic River at New Milford.

Railroad Street, New Milford.

The art deco Bank Street Theater is a definitive icon of
New Milford's commercial district.

The ornate and rare lenticular iron bridge at Lover's Leap State Park in New Milford.

The view across the village green in New Milford invokes
the towns colonial roots.

Driving north out of New Milford you experience the sudden transition to the rural side of New England. The next town is Gaylordsville where a not-so-glamorous bridge marks the first point where Route 7 and the Housatonic River cross. At the Kent town line, signs alert you that the next 28 miles have been designated Scenic Road—and for good reason. Two more miles down the road you reach Bulls Bridge.

The modern single-span bridge at Gaylordsville is either the first or the last—depending on which way you are traveling along Route 7—time that the Route 7 roadway passes over the Housatonic River.

Sunrise on the Housatonic River just north of Bulls Bridge. In this three mile stretch into Kent, the road and the river run side-by-side separated only by the river bank and there are continuous views of the mountains to the west along the Connecticut-New York border.

52

Bulls Bridge to Lime Rock

Chances are you will never forget the first time that you drove this section of road. It truly is that beautiful. The season of choice would be fall—after all, this is New England.

Like Gaylordsville, Bulls Bridge is little more than a crossroads. It does, however, have many charming characteristics. There is a friendly picture-postcard inn, and just to the west of the road is the first covered bridge that you will encounter along Route 7. This is the location of the Schaghticoke Indian Reservation and there a numerous pleasant trails that can be hiked through the surrounding hillsides. The Appalachian Trail also makes its first foray into New England here.

The covered bridge at Bulls Bridge is set over a shallow ravine where the river has been diverted at several points as part of the engineering for the complex of hydroelectric power systems that helped create Candlewood Lake. The water runs through vigorous rapids here and it a favorite spot for anglers.

The original course of the Housatonic River went through this channel where it cut its way through the limestone bedrock and left a maze of wildly shaped rocks and potholes.

54

An exotic reflection at sunrise on the Housatonic River in Kent.

At the best times of year the short stretch of road from Bulls Bridge up to Kent can be breathtaking. Route 7 hugs the banks of the river and there are beautiful views of the mountains off to the west along the border with New York. As you approach the town of Kent proper, the river veers off slightly to the west and the village welcomes you with its bountiful nurseries, antique shops, galleries, boutiques, and restaurants. Route 7 is the one principal road through town and for eight or ten blocks it makes up the commercial district. A few blocks west of the Civil War obelisk that stands at the only traffic light in town, and across the Housatonic, is Kent School.

Kent was settled and incorporated in 1738 and 1739 and was named for the county of Kent in England. Over the last 270 years the town has managed to retain a placid, understated character that has made it a thriving artists' colony. Shops and businesses are locally owned and the only symbol of massive-scale franchised corporate America is the gas station at the traffic light. Given the absence of big boxes, fast food joints, and convenience stores, it would be easy to imagine that you were standing in a different county altogether.

Kent Greenhouse is one of the first businesses that greets visitors entering Kent from the south on Route 7.

An eye-catching sculpted fountain in Kent.

View of North Main Street, Kent, from near the Civil War monument.

The First Congregational Church in Kent.

Kent is the perfect place to pause from the unbroken march north on Route 7 and explore some of the surrounding region of the Litchfield Hills. A series of back roads provides a perfect scenic loop that passes through the hamlet of New Preston and nearby Lake Waramaug.

The detour takes you through rolling farmland, around Hatch Pond and into South Kent before heading off to the east for several miles on the way to New Preston. Along the way you will enjoy open hilly countryside, a historic stone church, and some beautiful vistas.

This loop works particularly well because the preferred return leg back to Route 7 hooks up at Bulls Bridge and allows you to enjoy the drive back into Kent one more time.

A rural scene on South Kent Road heading toward South Kent and New Preston.

Hatch Pond in South Kent.

Opposite page
This view of the Housatonic Valley south of Kent is taken from a cluster of boulders just off the Appalachian Trail that is traditionally painted each year by the graduating class of Kent School. The colorful paintings make it visible from the road from a distance of several miles. Near the center of the picture a small slice of the Housatonic just beyond Kent School can be seen and Route 7 is visible along the far side of a clearing in the middle of the frame. The downtown area of Kent, set amongst the trees, occupies the left side of the frame.

59

The waterfall in New Preston.

Quintessential view of the Litchfield Hills on the road to New Preston.

Kent Falls State Park occupies 295 acres on the mountainside east of Route 7. It is one of the oldest state parks in Connecticut and has long been a favorite place for writers, artists, tourists and local folk. On its short journey west to the Housatonic River, Falls Brook reaches the mountain's edge and makes a 250 foot descent in a quarter mile over several sections of the falls that can be reached by a series of trails.

A large part of the appeal of Kent, for the passing traveler and the resident alike, is the access to its two state parks—Macedonia Brook and Kent Falls. Macedonia Brook State Park is directly west of town and has more than 2,000 acres to explore on a network of established trials. Some of them have beautiful views of nearby Taconic and Catskill mountain ranges in New York state.

The smaller and more intimate Kent Falls State Park is also known in Connecticut as "The Jewel of the Inland Parks." It is a favorite spot for picnickers and day-trippers from the metropolitan New York region and parts of New England.

A reproduction covered bridge acts as a gateway to Kent Falls State Park.

This page and the next three pages: Scenes from the side of the road in Cornwall, Connecticut, on the section of road from Kent Falls to Cornwall Bridge.

Before leaving the village of Kent you can also visit the Sloane Stanley and Kent Furnace Museum where the exhibits focus on outdoors exploration and the history of the local iron industry.

The road rises up on the way out of Kent and the next ten miles to Covered Bridge become an undulating journey through forests, into open valleys with expansive views, and down again to the river which it crisscrosses again just the beyond the roadside village of Cornwall Bridge. North of Cornwall Bridge you can enjoy the tranquility of Housatonic Meadows State Park, part of which is sandwiched between Route 7 and the Housatonic River for almost the entire 4-mile stretch to Covered Bridge. The park expands far up into the hills on either side of the river, but the areas along the river are undoubtedly the best it has to offer.

Housatonic Meadows is a popular and very welcome resting place for hikers on the Appalachian Trail. It is also a prime fly-fishing area. The tall pines of the park's forest seem to absorb the noise of passing traffic so that along the river, just a few hundred yards away, all you can hear is the gurgling of the Housatonic rushing over scattered boulders and rocks. There are canoe and kayak rentals available nearby as well as some rustic but comfortable accommodations.

In Cornwall Bridge, as Route 7 enters into the town of Sharon, it crosses both the Housatonic River and Connecticut Route 4.

This chapel is tucked away below the bridge on a triangle of land set on the river bank. It is rarely noticed by passersby.

While the covered bridge at Bulls Bridge is obscured from sight in a ravine just off the road, it is hard to miss the bright red, 172-foot covered bridge in West Cornwall.

Housatonic Meadows State Park

View of West Cornwall covered bridge from the river bank to the northeast.

Shops and signs in West Cornwall village.

Covered Bridge from the turn-off on Route 7.

Route 7 meanders through a tight thickly-wooded section for another four miles before emerging into open country at the intersection with Route 112, and once again crossing over the river. Lime Rock Race Track is less than a mile up 112, and you do have the option here of taking another short detour into the neighboring villages of Sharon, Lakeville, and Salisbury. There are myriad possible ways of looping back to Route 7 without missing more than a few miles of it; one of these is the beautiful Salmon Kill/Brinton Hill Road route east out of Salisbury that takes you to Falls Village.

White picket fences like this one on the village green in Sharon, Connecticut, are icons of New England.

These two trees create excellent subject matter for a landscape. I had passed them dozens of times before stopping on this frigid morning to try my luck at a good shot.

The aptly-named Grandview Farm is on the north side of Sharon overlooking Mudge Pond and the Taconic Range in New York.

The view south over Mudge Pond from the shoulder of Route 41 in Sharon.

Cemetery off of Route 4 in Sharon.

Lime Rock to North Canaan

Staying on Route 7 you arrive at Falls Village, which is a part of greater Canaan, in a mile or so. Since Falls Village was originally the epicenter of growth and prosperity for the whole area of what is now Canaan, both names are often used to describe the same place. Like a number of the previous villages along the way, Falls Village is tucked away on the bank of the Housatonic and it owes its existence to the particular features of the river that gave it commercial and industrial significance. The strong cascading water at Falls Village made it an attractive location for a sawmill and a gristmill in 1741. An iron works was built in 1743 and it provided machinery, weaponry, and components of infrastructure for both the Revolutionary and Civil Wars. All of the heavy industry has long since disappeared, but a power plant built between 1912 and 1913 is still in operation. Today Canaan is a relatively quiet town with limited light industry, substantial open pit mining activities, and a large pharmaceutical plant.

Pastoral scenes in Falls Village.

Opposite page
The large red barn at White Hollows Farms is a prominent element of the landscape at the intersection of Routes 7 and 112.

Pastoral scenes in Falls Village.

The drive from Falls Village to the center of North Canaan is another five miles and passes through beautiful countryside at the base of Canaan Mountain Natural Area Preserve. There are several areas of wetlands with gracefully rounded mountains as their backdrop and it is possible to hike trails to exposed ledges on the mountainside that offer up spectacular 180-degree views of the Housatonic Valley.

As you approach the first traffic light in town, Lower Road, to the right, leads to the Land of Nod Winery and the Beckley Furnace Industrial Monument Historic Preserve with its pleasant park along the Blackberry River, a tributary of the Housatonic. The modest business district of Canaan features an assortment of small businesses, some cafes, and the historic Colonial Theatre.

Falls Village Inn was originally designed as an Italianate building but was completely renovated in Queen Ann style at the turn of the 19th century. Over a period of 165 years, and through a succession of more than 15 different owners, the inn has served stage coach, train, and automobile travelers.

The girders of the steel bridge over the Housatonic in Falls Village frame the power plant.

The view from the ledges above Route 7 in Canaan are breathtaking. In this photograph the farm at the junction of Sand and Boinay Hill Roads catches sunrise light with the autumn-colored southern peaks of Mt. Riga State Park as a backdrop. Directly below is the Robbins Swamp Wildlife Management Area.

Sunrise over the Robbins
Swamp Wildlife Manage-
ment Area in Canaan at the
junction of Routes 7 & 63.

One of the many historic barns
on the side of the road.

Litchfield County, Connecticut, and the southern portion of Berkshire County, Massachusetts, combined to make up one of the first centers of the American iron industry. The earliest forges in this area date to the 1730s. The Beckley Furnace was built in the mid-1700s by industry pioneer Samuel Forbes and was one of the principal ironworks that created jobs, prosperity, and explosive growth for Falls Village/Canaan in the 18th and 19th centuries. Forbes and his partners built additional forges in the area including one in Lakeville. His iron works created standardized ships anchors that were bought by customers as far away as Philadelphia. Without these furnaces the country would have had a difficult time meeting its armaments and materiel needs for the Revolutionary War, the War of 1812, and the Civil War.

Man-made falls on the Blackberry River at the Beckley Furnace site.

82

As you come into the village of Canaan an unassuming sign directs you to the Land of Nod Winery on Lower Road. This is the northernmost vineyard on the Connecticut Wine Trail. It is run by the friendly Adams family and produces traditional grape-based wines as well as fruit-based varietals.

The authentic Collins Diner, in the center of North Canaan/ Falls Village, is an institution in the town and is one of Route 7's roadside slices of Americana.

The view from the ledges on Canaan Mountain looking north into Massachusetts through the Housatonic River valley.

Ironically, two of the last things you see on the west side of Route 7 as you leave Connecticut are the State Trooper Barracks followed almost immediately by this sign for the liquor store. For some reason I have always liked this weather-beaten sign.

Twin Lakes, a popular boating destination, is set in a bowl to the west of Canaan at the base of Mt. Riga State Park.

There are so many scenes similar to this one that you can find throughout the Berkshires if you have enough time to ferret them out. I was on my way somewhere else to photograph sunrise when I caught this out of the corner of my eye, hit the brakes, and spun back around.

Massachusetts

Ashley Falls to Great Barrington

Of the three states that Route 7 passes through, Massachusetts requires the shortest length of road by far. It is just 55 miles from the border in Ashley Falls, a village of Sheffield, to the Vermont border just north of Williamstown. All of those 55 miles pass through Berkshire County, which takes up the entire western end of Massachusetts and borders three states. Curiously, the name Ethan Allen Highway does not appear on any of the signage for Route 7 in Massachusetts and it is not subtitled this way on any map that I have found.

However, it is fair to say that Berkshire County is more densely packed with attractions and points of interest than any other section of the road. It has been called "Americas Premier Cultural Resort," and for good reason. Over the last thirty years, building on a solid foundation, the Berkshires has become a cultural mecca of world-class museums, international film festivals, summer stock theatre companies, concert venues, art galleries, lecture series, and much more.

To be sure, long before all of this began to flourish, the Berkshires already had such long-standing institutions as Tanglewood (the summer home of the Boston Symphony), The Berkshire Museum, Jacob's Pillow, The Sterling and Francine Clark Art Institute, and the Berkshire Theatre Festival, but beginning in the 1980s the rapid growth of its economy brought unprecedented sources of capital and funding into the area and promoted significant expansions of the existing venues *and* a proliferation of new organizations.

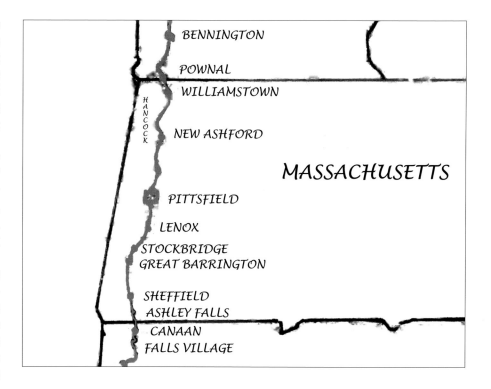

The journey through the Berkshires begins in Ashley Falls where the Housatonic valley opens out into a wide, shallow bowl the serves up beautiful distant views of the landscape right from the front seat of your car. The newer section of Route 7 is, however, a relatively sterile stretch of road, so it is highly advisable to take 7A en route to Sheffield. This is the first section of 7A that one encounters on the way north and it gives you the opportunity to visit Bartholomew's Cobble, a bucolic hillside preserve that rises up from the banks of the Housatonic and provides excellent views of the whole valley to the north and Mt. Ev-erett State Forest to the west. The Colonel John Ashley house, which was discussed earlier in this book, is also just a few hundred yards from the welcome hut at Bartholomew's Cobble.

Once off of the main road there are actually three choices of parallel roads that lead to Sheffield. Route 7A and Ranapo Road run essentially side by side, but, on the other side of Route 7, Hewins Street is undoubtedly the most scenic option as it curves and dips through the surrounding farmland.

The Housatonic River in Ashley Falls near Bartholomew's Cobble and the Colonel John Ashley house.

Every year the Howden Farm in Ashley Falls creates a hay bale maze and seasonal display for their pumpkin farm. Howden Farm is located on Ranapo Road, one of the two roads that run parallel to Route 7 and act as alternatives to driving a featureless section of the main road.

Ashley Falls.

Howden Farm, Ashley Falls.

The other, even more desirable, alternative route for the stretch from Ashley Falls to Sheffield is Hewins Road, which follows a mild roller coaster path along the Housatonic River and has wonderful views of Mt. Everett State Forest.

Sheffield, the oldest town in all of Berkshire County, is four miles north of Ashley Falls. Over time the look of the town has remained remarkably constant and the roadside aesthetics have never been compromised by billboards and neon. Like Kent, Sheffield is built up on either side of Route 7 and the dominant commercial elements are the antique shops that line the road at both ends of town. In the center of town there is a cutout on the west side of Route 7 that provides access to a row of shops, cafes, churches, and the post office.

First Congregational Church on the cutout in the center of Sheffield.

One of the many whimsical small businesses you will pass along Route 7 is the Red Hen on the north side of Sheffield.

On the north side of Sheffield you can visit the site of what was the oldest covered bridge in Massachusetts. The original bridge was built in 1854 and was in use until 1974 when it was closed to all vehicular traffic. In 1981 extensive preservation work was done to ensure that the bridge would remain a popular local attraction and a monument to the era of covered bridges. Unfortunately it burned to the ground in 1994. The current bridge is an authentic reproduction that was built in 1998.

North of Sheffield and into Great Barrington, Route 7 is predominantly commercial, which again presents the opportunity for a short detour that, in this case, would favor the Sheffield-Egremont Road. The road knifes off of Route 7 just beyond the covered bridge and borders a dairy farm before jumping a small hill and entering a gorgeous valley. The last battle of Shay's Rebellion took place in a field just beyond an intersection in the middle of the valley.

From the Shay's Rebellion monument the Sheffield-Egremont Road rolls past several farms before gliding into the historic town center of Egremont. The main road in town is Route 23 and the detour can be completed by taking Route 23 east back to the intersection with Route 7 at the south end of Great Barrington.

The rebuilt covered bridge in Sheffield.

The Housatonic just upriver from the Sheffield covered bridge.

If you choose to explore any one of the secondary roads that parallel Route 7 from Ashley Falls to Sheffield, you are almost certain to come across a scene like this.

The Delmolino farm on the Sheffield-Egremont Road has always been one of my favorite locations in all of the Berkshires. The farm and the surrounding landscape is beautiful from every angle and in every season.

Shay's Rebellion was one of the first cases of armed civil unrest in the history of the United States. Battling crippling taxes that were bankrupting small farmers and prompting repossessions of their land by the government, a militia of western Massachusetts farmers took on the newly formed army. While the uprising failed, it did prompt the Constitutional Convention of 1787.

Great Barrington was incorporated in 1761 and was, like Sheffield, primarily an agricultural town until the mid-1800s. Railroads came to Great Barrington in 1842 and soon substantial mills were being built in both Great Barrington and the village of Housatonic.

1842 was also the first year of the Barrington Fair, which had been proposed a year earlier at the founding of the Housatonic Agricultural Society. The Fair would go on to become one of the region's premier annual events and ran continuously until 1984, after which there was a series of interruptions until it finally closed for good in 1998.

After the Civil War there was another boost of prosperity when the elite of New York and Boston began taking an interest in the Berkshires as a summer resort. Around the turn of the 20th century electric street lights and trolleys ran the length of Main Street and the commercial district of town had assumed its present-day look with attractive rows of three-story brick commercial buildings. By the 1970s and 1980s, however, the town's polish had worn off a bit.

I think it is safe to say that there is no other town along the entire length of Route 7 that has experienced a more staggering reversal of fortune over the last 30 years than Great Barrington. Beginning around 1990 a group of concerned local citizens and business people formed the Main Street Action Association to seek a variety of ways, and the necessary capital, to revitalize the downtown. Almost twenty years later is it clear that their efforts bore considerable fruit as Great Barrington is now the hub of the southern Berkshires. Today there are about fifty restaurants in this town of only 8,500 people, and its storefronts are filled with an eclectic mix of stylish boutiques, specialty stores, and prestigious art galleries. Sometime in the last ten years the nickname "Little SoHo" was coined and it has resonated with both the travel press and visitors.

The long and storied run of the Barrington Fairgrounds concluded abruptly in 1998 when the owner of the property ended a dispute with the townspeople over off-track betting at the facility and decided to put it up for sale. The Fairgrounds had long been the home of the Berkshire County Fair and a popular horse racing track but, apparently, had been losing money for years. Not much has been resolved in the last ten years and the building has become an overgrown ghost. With Monument Mountain looming over the grandstand in the background, it is an unmistakable landmark as you enter Great Barrington from Sheffield.

The elegant Wainwright Inn is a fine example of the many restored inns and B&B's that welcome travelers up and down Route 7.

Every spring, around the first week of May, Great Barrington's Main Street (Route 7) sidewalks acquire a blazing white canopy as the pear blossom trees explode from their winter slumber.

The Mason Library is another example of the types of civic projects that are being undertaken to rehabilitate town centers and precious historic landmarks throughout the Route 7 corridor.

The countryside around Great Barrington can only be described as quintessentially New England.

Scenes of rural life abound in the countryside around Great Barrington.

Housatonic is a village within the township of Great Barrington. It is typical of mill towns all over New England that have had to devise increasingly more creative solutions to the decline of their core economies.

Great Barrington to Lenox

Route 7 leaves Great Barrington through a gauntlet of commercial establishments and restaurants and then begins the ascent of the lower slopes of Monument Mountain, past Fountain Pond State Park and the parking lot for the Monument trail heads, and on through a vast swath of wetlands. Next stop, Stockbridge, adopted home of Norman Rockwell.

Squaw Peak on Monument Mountain is framed by a branch of apple blossoms in this view from Windy Hill Farm's orchards.

Fountain Pond State Park is at the top of the initial rise Route 7 makes north of Great Barrington. Although it is easy to miss, it has a large cutout parking area on the side of the road and is a popular rest area, fishing hole, and bird watching location.

Opposite page
Monument Mountain is to the southern region of Route 7, what Mt. Philo, in Charlotte, Vermont, is to the northern region. Over centuries it made its way into the history of the native people as well as the generations of European settlers and immigrants who came to America. It has some of the most popular hiking trails in the Berkshires if not along the whole length of Route 7. This view from near Squaw Peak looks north over Agawam Lake Wildlife Management Area toward Stockbridge and Lenox. Route 7 is visible cutting through the picture from the right, and Mt. Greylock appears on the horizon.

Ski Butternut is the first significant ski area you will encounter along Route 7. There is the much smaller Mohawk Mountain Ski Area a few miles off of Route 7 in Litchfield County, and the more challenging Catamount is about eight miles west of Great Barrington, but Butternut, with its renowned family orientation, seems to have the broadest appeal.

102

It is difficult to say whether Stockbridge owes its success to Norman Rockwell or vice versa. In truth, their relationship was purely symbiotic and they both benefited enormously from the association. Furthermore, it is also difficult to overstate how much Stockbridge means today to the Berkshires and the rest of the region that Route 7 serves. The enduring ideals that Rockwell expressed through his paintings are also reflected in the fact that Stockbridge has managed so successfully to preserve the historic image of main street America. The fact that the town has changed so little over the last 100 years greatly facilitates its annual transformation in December to the famous scene that Rockwell painted with vintage cars parked outside of the Main Street storefronts. All of these things draw hundreds of thousands of visitors to Stockbridge every year and many of them then fan out into the rest of the Berkshires and the surrounding states from there. The permanent monument to this unique relationship between a man and a small town is the meticulous Norman Rockwell Museum which was awarded the prestigious National Humanities Medal in 2008.

The Red Lion dressed up for Christmas.

The Red Lion corner must be one of the most famous intersections in the Berkshires, not only because it handles so much of the traffic moving in either direction through the Berkshires, but also because it oozes the Rockwellian vision of Main Street America. This unique vantage point takes in the civil war monument across the street.

For twenty years the Stockbridge Main Street At Christmas, which began in 1990, has been one of the most popular events of the winter season. Stockbridge's Main Street is closed off and the scene Rockwell painted from 1956 to 1967 is recreated.

Norman Rockwell's studio on the grounds of the Norman Rockwell Museum in Stockbridge.

The view north from Rockwell's studio.

Main Street, Stockbridge.

Passing time on a summer afternoon on the porch of the Red Lion Inn is a rite of passage for so many people who visit the Berkshires each year.

Of course, there is much more to Stockbridge that beckons visitors. Chesterwood, the home and studio of Daniel Chester French, sculptor of the Lincoln Memorial, is a serene retreat with wooded trails and sweeping views of October Mountain State Forest. The unpretentious Berkshire Botanical Garden is a wonderful place to spend an hour or two strolling around. The renowned Berkshire Theatre Festival, which boasts some of the most exceptional talent available, has operated in Stockbridge for 80 years and is the oldest continuously-running cultural venue in the Berkshires. And there are great outdoor recreational possibilities with Stockbridge Bowl and the countless hills, mountains, valleys, rivers, lakes, fields, golf courses, and sporting facilities that surround you.

The Housatonic River turns away from Route 7 after the point where they cross just south of town and passes through South Lee, Lee, and Lenox Dale, staying east of Route 7 all the way up to Pittsfield where it splits into an east and a west branch.

View of Daniel Chester French's studio, where he designed the Lincoln Memorial, through the hydrangea walk. Chesterwood is one of the gems of the Berkshires considerable portfolio of cultural attractions.

In 2008 the Berkshire Theatre Festival celebrated its 80th year of operations.

The fountain in front of French's studio door.

The Stockbridge Bowl boat launch on Route 183.

Looking south to Monument Mountain from Gould Meadow across the street from the Tanglewood grounds.

The summer events sponsored by the Colonial Carriage & Driving Society include the biannual carriage driving parade through the country roads of the Berkshires, complete with the pageantry of the Gilded Age.

The formal gardens at Edith Wharton's The Mount Estate and Gardens.

Relative to the towns of Sheffield, Great Barrington, and Stockbridge, Lenox was a late bloomer. It wasn't settled until 1750 and it grew slowly for its first 100 years despite the fact that it had become the county seat in 1784, beating out Great Barrington and Pittsfield for the distinction (the county seat was turned back to Pittsfield in 1871). However, as with Great Barrington, the Gilded Age of the late 1800s ushered in a period of dramatic change for the town from which it has never looked back. The hilly land between Stockbridge and Lenox became some of the most desirable in America and a silent competition between the two towns to woo the era's super-wealthy from Boston and New York simmered for years. And while both towns prospered, it was Lenox that became known as the "inland Newport."[18]

The catalyst for Lenox's ascendancy among the intellectual, cultural, and financial elite of the nation was the relocation of one family to Lenox from Stockbridge in 1821. When Charles Sedgwick took the job of town clerk and moved to Lenox with his wife Elizabeth, his sister Catherine, one of America's first well-known female writers, joined them. Catherine was well connected with the country's cultural elite and was, in particular, close friends with Fanny Kemble. Kemble began her association with Lenox as a frequent guest of Sedgwick's and soon purchased land and built an estate named "The Perch." Word quickly spread about this burgeoning hill town in the Berkshires and a wave of migration of writers, actors, intellectuals, and other people of power and influence ensued. By the end of the 19th century Lenox had, in one way or another, been the place of residence for such prominent names as Nathaniel Hawthorne, Edith Wharton, Andrew Carnegie, George Westinghouse, and Margaret Vanderbilt.[19]

The wealth in turn created a demand for hospitality, entertainment, and cultural venues and, as this infrastructure reached an opulent scale, an elite resort community was born. Through two world wars and the cyclical economic vagaries of the 20th century Lenox has endured as a premier destination.

The countryside west of Route 7 between Stockbridge and Lenox, which is essentially the valley of Stockbridge Bowl between Rattlesnake and West Stockbridge mountains, is part of the loop of Route 183. This is a beautiful side road that parallels Route 7 along the Housatonic River through the Village of Housatonic and Glendale, and passes by Chesterwood, the Norman Rockwell Museum, The Berkshire Bo-

tanical Gardens, Stockbridge Bowl, and Tanglewood before rejoining Route 7A in the center of Lenox. Doing a full circuit of Routes 183 and 7 from Great Barrington to Lenox is by far the best way to enjoy and appreciate this unique section of the Route 7 corridor. Leaving Lenox by way of Route 7A takes you through the historic center of Lenox past the Church on the Hill and is a way of avoiding the short stretch of the Lenox bypass.

Up and down Route 7 many Gilded Age mansions, like Cranwell, have been preserved as exclusive resorts.

112

Unlike Lenox, the town of Lee has always maintained a more down-to-earth nature and it was never affected to the same degree by the excesses of the Gilded Age. Norman Rockwell choose Lee as fodder for a number of his paintings because of its understated, working-class ethic and, in September, 2008, ABC television's "Good Morning America" began the brief Berkshires leg of their 50-state pre-election whistle-stop tour of the country outside of Joe's Diner, the setting of one of Rockwell's most famous paintings.

Tyringham Valley is not exactly on Route 7, but it is one of the most intimate valleys in the Berkshires and is well worth the effort of making the roughly 10-mile detour through Lee to get there.

One last, unique look at The Mount.

The former County Court House now serves as the much beloved Lenox Library. The cupola was restored, to much delight, in 2006-7.

Main Street (Route 7A) in Lenox.

Spring time in Lenox.

The iconic Church on the Hill on Route 7A in Lenox.

This winter scene of a residential street in Lenox was taken at an intersection on Route 7.

The Cornell Inn is one of the many well kept inns and B&B's in Lenox.

The sprawling campus property of Shakespeare & Company on Kemble Street in Lenox (named for Fanny Kemble) is part of the venerable theatre company's appeal to tourists.

Winter on the side roads around Lenox.

Lenox to Pittsfield

Pittsfield, with a population of about 45,000, is the only city in the Berkshires. Predictably, it is more ethnically diverse than the many small towns of the region and it is the industrial and economic center of Berkshire County.

The city was first settled in 1752, and, like Great Barrington and Sheffield, progressed as a small agricultural town with some light industry until the beginning of the 1800s.

The aesthetic qualities of Stockbridge and Lenox bled over into Pittsfield which, while it built a far more diverse economic foundation through the early and mid-1800s, also attracted some of America's cultural titans like Henry Wadsworth Longfellow, Oliver Wendell Holmes, and Herman Melville, who wrote *Moby Dick* while living on his farmstead on Pittsfield's east side. As this book was being written, a proposal to designate *Moby Dick* the Official Book of Massachusetts was put to the state legislature.

The importation of merino sheep from Spain, beginning in 1807, gave birth to a thriving wool manufacturing industry in Pittsfield. The city became the dominant player in the country's woolens industry for the next 75-100 years.[20]

But Pittsfield's real transformation from an agriculturally-based economy to a heavy industrial manufacturing center occurred in the 1890s, when William Stanley, who had famously brought electric streetlights to Great Barrington, moved his Electric Manufacturing Company to Pittsfield from Great Barrington and produced the first electric transformer in his new plant. This would eventually create mixed consequences for the city. In 1902 the Stanley Electric Manufacturing Company was absorbed into General Electric. For most of the 20th century GE would become, in a sense, the corporate parent of Pittsfield, employing over 10,000 workers and fueling a period of prosperity from roughly 1940-1980. The last thirty years have witnessed first a gradual shrinking of GE's operations in Pittsfield and finally the outright sale of them. This, in turn, has forced the city to remake itself.

Since this book deals with road and automobile travel, it seems fitting to make mention of an obscure Berkshire native whose invention that was born in a small shop in Pittsfield had a profound impact on the driving experience. George Shippey left his job at the Stanley Electric Manufacturing Company sometime in the early 1900s and produced the "Shippey Spring" which he patented in 1906 and eventually modified to become the first shock absorber.[21]

Over the past ten years Pittsfield's elected leaders have made significant strides in diversifying the industrial and manufacturing base and reinvigorating its central business district. In 2005 Barrington Stage Company relocated to Pittsfield and economic incentive grants have allowed the city to build a new transportation center and a multiplex movie theatre. But the symbolic culmination of all these efforts to date was the completion of the full restoration of The Colonial Theatre in 2006. The project saw a cultural sleeping giant reawakened and it has brought a wide range of entertainment and cultural events back to Pittsfield.

Route 7 leads directly to Park Square in the center of Pittsfield, passing the venerable Berkshire Life Insurance Building, Pittsfield Country Club, The Colonial Theatre, and Berkshire Museum along the way. The most appealing route through the city is to circle around the park and continue on North Street through the commercial district rejoining Route 7 across from Berkshire Medical Center. The road then snakes through Pittsfield's northern neighborhoods before encountering Pontoosuc Lake. As you begin to skirt the east shore of the lake you get your first distant glimpse of Mount Greylock, Massachusetts's tallest mountain at 3,491 feet above sea level.

Pittsfield City Hall.

Summers in Pittsfield are punctuated by Third Thursdays street festivals held on the third Thursday of each month from May through October.

The proscenium, the classic ceiling relief, and the two upper seating galleries
of the Colonial Theatre can be seen here in all of their restored glory.

The Berkshire Museum has benefited enormously from Pittsfield's downtown revitalization efforts of the last ten years.

Each July 4th, on the morning before the parade, Pittsfield stages a charity run down North Street.

The parade makes it way up North Main Street.

Spectators at Pittsfield's July 4th parade, which is one of the largest in the country.

The modern part of Pittsfield's downtown business district seen from the intersection of West and Center Streets.

Right and opposite page
One block south of The Colonial Theatre in Pittsfield is the intersection with Route 20 which provides access to Hancock Shaker Village about two miles west of the city. The round barn at Hancock Shaker Village was revolutionary in its time and is one of The Berkshires most popular cultural attractions.

Pittsfield to Williamstown

Route 7 passes through Lanesborough and New Ashford on the way to Williamstown. In Lanesborough, N. Main Street, which eventually becomes Greylock Road, cuts off to the right and leads up to the summit of Mt. Greylock. Among the many points of interest is the fact that Mt. Greylock State Reservation is home to the only know stand of old growth red spruce left in New England.

The main road follows a narrow valley between Saddle Ball Mountain (part of Mt. Greylock State Reservation) to the east and Brodie Mountain to the west and has few side roads for the next fifteen miles. There are some pleasant and fleeting views to the north, but overall this does not rank as one of the more scenic sections of Route 7. In light of that, a more appealing alternative is to turn off on Brodie Mountain Road and drive over a mountain pass to Route 43 in Hancock, turn right and follow Route 43 all the way to Five Corners in South Williamstown.

Jiminy Peak ski area in Hancock has transformed itself into a four-season resort built on a green energy platform using electricity generated by a windmill that was installed near the mountain's peak in 2007. The successful project has gained wide exposure and considerable acclaim.

The memorial tower at the summit of Mt. Greylock has magnificent views well into the Pioneer Valley of central Massachusetts.

Opposite page
Twilight over Pontoosuc Lake, the largest lake on Route 7 in Massachusetts.

Jiminy Peak can be seen from the road side of Route 43, which makes for a beautiful detour from Route 7 in all seasons.

Hancock Town hall with Jiminy Peak's Zephyr windmill on the mountain ridge in the background.

A dramatic sunset performs a light show extravaganza on the hillsides of Hancock.

Sunrise on Route 43 in Hancock.

Although Five Corners is nothing more than an intersection, it does have a number of significant distinguishing attributes. The most obvious of these is the Store at Five Corners which occupies the site of the first log cabin built in the hamlet in 1762. Second is the very popular market and produce stand at Green River Farms, adjacent to the store. Diagonally across Route 7 is the beloved Waubeeka Golf Links. Constructed in 1966 and 1967, the course, with its panoramic views of Mt Greylock and all of the surrounding peaks, is widely considered to be one of the most beautiful in New England. In early 2008 the club was put up for sale and there was loud public outcry over speculation that it would fall prey to developers if it were sold. Fortunately, Jim Goff, a native son of Williamstown, avid golfer, and prominent businessman eventually purchased it with a long-term commitment to improve and preserve the course.

However, the main attraction of Five Corners is the view from the top of the hill above the intersection. From this point there is a sweeping vista of all of Mt. Greylock State Reservation, the pastoral valleys south of Williamstown, and the Green Mountains to the north. Throughout the year, but especially in summer and fall, on any day of the week, it is common to see several cars pulled to side of the road so that their occupants could step out and snap photographs. Chances are you'll want to do the same.

One of the countless views toward Mt. Greylock from the fairways and greens of Waubeeka Golf Links in South Williamstown.

The Store at Five Corners.

The Green River just off of Route 7 in South Williamstown.

The grand vista from the top of the hill above Five Corners must be one of the most photographed places in all of western New England. The Memorial Tower at the peak of Mount Greylock appears on the ridge line in the center of this photograph.

The view looking northeast from the hilltop above Five Corners.

A pair of bicyclists stop to take in the view.

Route 7 drops down into the narrow valley of Hemlock Brook for the final few miles into Williamstown proper. The focal point of the town, of course, is Williams College. Williams is consistently credited as being one of the foremost small liberal arts colleges in the entire United States. Were it not for Colonel Ephraim Williams, a wealthy veteran of the Revolutionary War and one of the first settlers, there would not be a Williams College, and Williamstown would almost certainly be a different town today. In a great gesture borne out of his core benevolence and considerable generosity, and laced with a substantial portion of self-indulgence, Williams set aside a sum of money in his will to fund the construction of a school so long as his name would be applied to both the town and the college. Thus he created two permanent monuments to his time on earth.[22] The school nickname, the Ephs, is even derived from his first name, and, while this may not be due to any directive from him, it shows the depth to which his legacy is embedded in the culture of the school.

Williams College.

Griffin Hall, one of the most impressive buildings on the Williams College campus.

A unique view up Spring Street, the business district of Williamstown.

The tree-lined streets of Williamstown are quintessentially "New England."

The Williams College '62 Center for Theatre and Dance was completed in 2005 and is the home of the Williamstown Theatre Festival.

The Sterling And Francine Clark Art Institute in Williamstown, better known as The Clark, not only has a world-class art collection, but rivals the Frick in New York and the Getty Museum in Malibu for the unique character of its buildings and their surroundings. The Clark has fostered a philosophy that embraces the beauty of its substantial hillside property as a component of the experience of visiting the museum. It has worked closely both as a collaborator and consultant on numerous projects with other museums in the area as was the case with the celebrated Sol Lewitt permanent exhibit at Mass MoCA in North Adams.

Gallery 2 at The Clark, commonly referred to as "The Impressionist Gallery," is home to the museum's impressionist collection. With its frosted glass ceiling that diffuses the outside sunlight this gallery has a unique atmosphere.

Sterling and Francine Clark were two other prominent benefactors of Williamstown. The Clarks collected art in Paris in the early 1900s and in 1950 decided to create a permanent public home for their extensive holdings. The result was the impeccable Sterling and Francine Clark Art Institute which has grown to become one of the most revered art museums in the world. The museum plays an active role in the daily life of Williamstown and has worked in support of, and in collaboration with, the Williams College Museum of Art as well as other prominent cultural institutions around the world.

Williamstown is blessed with beautiful topography, making it an outdoors paradise in addition to its educational and cultural assets.

The neighboring city of North Adams was thrust into the spotlight of the art world in 1999 with the opening of the Massachusetts Museum of Contemporary Art (Mass MoCA) in the sprawling abandoned mill buildings of the former Sprague Electric Company which abruptly shuttered its factory in 1985. This symbol of revival for the struggling city was the passion and vision of long–serving Mayor John Barrett III and took thirteen years to come to fruition. From the outset it has established a new standard for contemporary art museums around the world and its reputation was further cemented in 2008 with the unveiling of the Sol Lewitt exhibit to widespread critical acclaim.

The vision of Mayor John Barrett, and the focus of over ten years of his long career leading the city of North Adams, Mass MoCA has been a resounding success story for North Adams, the Berkshires, and Massachusetts. Each year it seems to reach new heights and is consistently praised in the national press.

The view from Cobble Hill above Williamstown takes in the village below and looks south over the Hemlock River Valley where Route 7 cuts its path at the base of the Taconic Range.

Vermont

Although there is continuity in the landscape as Route 7 crosses the border into Vermont, the look and feel of the man-made elements changes drastically. In contrast to the Berkshires, the landscape becomes much less densely populated and the distance between towns increases noticeably. The towns themselves often have a more rustic appearance, there are fewer roadside businesses, there is generally less traffic, and there are virtually no billboards. It is similar to the northern section of Route 7 beyond Bulls Bridge in Connecticut but on a larger scale.

Wherever it appears on maps of Vermont Route 7 regains its more formal name—Ethan Allen Highway—yet the absence of any signs acknowledging this along the road carries over from Massachusetts. But there is a noticeable improvement over both the Massachusetts and, to a lesser extent, Connecticut sections of the road in terms of the treatment of historical information. The Vermont Division For Historical Preservation deserves mention for the extensive and comprehensive nature of the prominent, artfully trimmed, green historic markers that appear at hundreds of locations along Route 7 and, most probably, throughout the state.

By far the largest portion of Route 7 is found in Vermont. From the southern border in Pownal to the Canadian border in Highgate Springs there are 180 miles of tarmac and concrete—more than twice the distance in Connecticut, and more than three times the distance in Massachusetts. For almost half of this distance, Route 7 passes through a deep narrow valley between the Green Mountains of central Vermont and the Taconic Range along the eastern border of New York. For the first 75 miles this makes for a very defined path and lots of dramatic scenery. Not far beyond Rutland the road reaches the plain of the Lake Champlain basin, slowly drifts away from the Green Mountains and becomes surprisingly flat and wide open.

The strategic and economic importance of Route 7 to Vermont cannot be overstated. All five of Vermont's largest cities and towns are strung along Route 7 and the road handles the vast majority of the flow of commerce and tourism into the state from northeastern New York state, New York City, and southwestern New England.

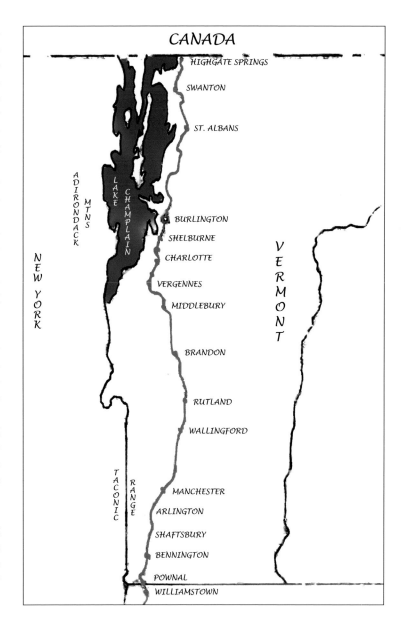

Pownal to Shaftsbury

As you leave the northern edge of Williamstown, Route 7 quickly begins to gain elevation as it climbs around Mason Hill and overlooks the picturesque Hoosic River valley and the town of Pownal. Until 1995, Pownal was home to the Green Mountain Greyhound Race Track. Since a ban on racing was put into effect that year the track facility had remained ominously dormant. In 2007 it was brought back to life when a consortium of local organizations organized the first annual Tri-State Fair.

From Pownal, Route 7 meanders through alternating pockets of residential neighborhoods and open country for several miles before dropping down into the center of Bennington. In 1749, Bennington became the first chartered town in Vermont when the Governor of the New Hampshire Territory, Benning Wentworth, signed the necessary documents and, literally, put his name on the map. However, the first actual settlers did not arrive in Bennington until 1761. Bennington's early history is similar to that of the many mill towns to the south along Route 7 that we have already explored. Building on such early mainstays as grist mills, saw mills, and iron works, the town went on to develop a strong textile industry that thrived for roughly 100 years. The 20th century saw a decline in the basic textile business and ushered a period of diversification to industries supplying automotive manufacturers and electronics.

The Hoosic River valley in Pownal viewed from the shoulder of Route 7.

The Tri-State Fair on the grounds of the defunct Green Mountain Race Track.

Display on R. Keith Armstrong's property in Pownal.

147

The reenactment of the Battle of Bennington.

But Bennington is clearly best known for the Battle of Bennington that actually took place across the state line in North Hoosick, New York, but has been boldly commemorated in Bennington since the completion of the Bennington Battle Monument in 1891.

The monument is an impressive structure that can be seen for miles from virtually every direction because of its location on the hilly slopes to the west of town. It is 306 feet high and has an observation level at about 200 feet. On a clear day it is possible to see the peak of Mount Greylock almost 20 miles to the south. Looking north through the valley that Route 7 follows the views stretch even further.

Today, with a population of roughly 15,000 Bennington is the fifth largest town in Vermont. Besides the Battle Monument it has a good assortment of other attractions including the Bennington Museum, the Covered Bridge Museum (another of the wonderfully esoteric museums that exist along Route 7), a classic colonial church with its adjoining cemetery, three nicely maintained and/or restored covered bridges—the most pleasant of which is the Henry Bridge—and a very civilized downtown of wide, tree-lined avenues. Near the Bennington Museum a historic marker indicates a point where the enigmatic "Corkscrew Railroad" passed through Bennington on its way to Troy, New York.

At the north end of Bennington, Route 7 splits forming the last of three sections of the road posted as 7A, or in this case, Historic 7A, to the east, and the new limited-access freeway section that bypasses the villages of Shaftsbury, Arlington, and Manchester as it hugs the western edge of the valley floor. Although there are occasional spectacular views from the new highway, the only way to truly enjoy the experience of driving Route 7 is to opt for Historic 7A.

The Bennington Monument viewed from Monument Avenue.

The graceful scalloping on the fence at the Old First Church frames the graveyard where Robert Frost is buried.

Right and opposite:
The streets of downtown Bennington.

The Hemmings Motor News building.

While gas stations aren't normally my choice of subject matter, the Hemmings station adjacent to the Motor News Building is a true piece of Americana and a symbol of the experience of car travel in this country.

The Henry Bridge northwest of downtown Bennington is a town-lattice structure with a 117-foot span that dates to 1840. It is the nicest of Bennington's three bridges.

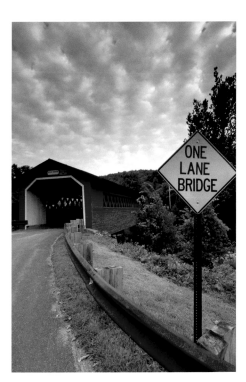

The 2008 Memorial Day Parade in Bennington.

The Bennington Museum

The commanding view from Bennington Monument looking toward Mt. Greylock.

The view from the shoulder of the modern freeway section of Route 7 in Sunderland.

Modern Route 7 in Manchester.

157

As you travel north on Historic 7A out of Bennington you begin a leisurely drive that snakes and dips through the rustic villages of South Shaftsbury and Shaftsbury en route to Arlington. In South Shaftsbury you can visit "Stone House," the home that Robert Frost purchased after selling his farm in Franconia, New Hampshire, and moving to Vermont in 1920. Frost spent most of the remainder of his life in Vermont during which time his career reached its peak as he was awarded four Pulitzer Prizes for his poetry. During this time he also cultivated his long and fulfilling relationship with Middlebury College and founded the retreat at Bread Loaf near the mountain village of Ripton. Frost was laid to rest alongside his wife in the cemetery of the Old Congregational Church in Bennington.

A small crowd gathered for a solemn ceremony at the graveyard in Shaftsbury on Memorial Day, 2008.

Robert Frost's "Stone House" in South Shaftsbury.

Shaftsbury to Wallingford

Arlington is an attractive village of colonial and Greek-revival houses set on either side of the road. Two notable former residents are commemorated here. Novelist and educator Dorothy Canfield Fisher lived most of her life in Arlington and Norman Rockwell lived here for twenty-three years before relocating to Stockbridge, Massachusetts. During the time he lived in Arlington, his career flourished. There is a modest museum dedicated to him in the village.

Half way between Arlington and Manchester Village you will encounter the Mount Equinox Skyline trail. It is the longest privately-owned paved toll road in the United States and its sole purpose is to transport you 3,248 feet over 5.2 miles of road to the summit of Mount Equinox. The views from the saddle are nothing short of breathtaking and this alone is worth the mild inconvenience of choosing 7A over the freeway.

The Arlington Dairy Bar on Route 7A provides a slice of Americana to go with your soft serve.

Haying in a field along Route 7A in Arlington.

Peonies in full bloom in the formal gardens at Robert Todd Lincoln's Hildene.

The next major attraction on 7A is Hildene, the elegant mountainside estate of Abraham Lincoln's son, Robert Todd Lincoln. Robert Todd Lincoln became wealthy as president of the Pullman Company and built his sumptuous mansion and gardens in 1905 at the peak of the Gilded Age. The property has magnificent views of the Battenkill Valley below.

Manchester Village and Manchester Center make up the first bustling tourist destination that you will encounter along Route 7 in Vermont. Anchored by the exclusive Equinox Resort and Spa, greater Manchester boasts dozens of hotels, inns, and B&B's. The town has been a prominent resort for most of its 200-plus years of existence. One of the attractions of the area is the abundance of prime fly-fishing ponds, lakes, and rivers. Manchester native Charles Orvis seized upon the opportunity he saw in this and began a fishing rod manufacturing business in 1856 that very soon afterward became the first mail order business in America. The Orvis Company still has its flagship location in Manchester, complete with a fully stocked trout pond where potential customers can take rods for a spin.

Not coincidentally, another of the esoteric museums I alluded to in an earlier chapter is located down the road from the Orvis store—The American Museum of Fly Fishing.

The northern neighborhoods of Manchester are set among rolling foothills where you can find beautiful iconic scenery and still more distant views of the main valley.

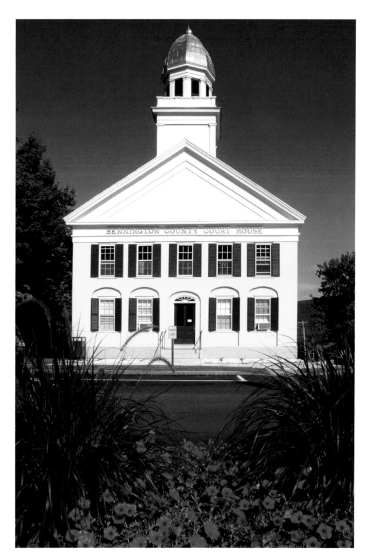

The gold-domed County Courthouse in Manchester village stands over the green opposite the Equinox Resort.

The Equinox Resort.

Fishing rod display at the Orvis store in Manchester.

Manchester Village.

162

Landscapes on the north side of Manchester Center.

The world-class four-season resort at Stratton Mountain is an easy 25 minute drive off of Route 7. Stratton is the first of Vermont's major ski areas that can be accessed from Route 7 as you travel north. There are no ski areas directly on Route 7 in Vermont.

164

Manchester serves as a gateway to two other attractions that are worthy of note. To the east, Route 30 climbs up the slopes of Spruce Peak in the direction of the ski areas of Bromley Mountain and Stratton Mountain. While both are popular ski destinations, Stratton has invested heavily since the 1980s to develop a world-class, four season resort that sports a 27-hole championship golf course set against the ski slopes.

In the other direction Route 30 leads west to Dorset. The first marble mines in America were opened in Dorset in 1785 and their output made the town prosperous in its infancy. The town came of age in the 1800s as both a spa and a burgeoning artists' colony. Just as with Lenox, Massachusetts, but on a smaller scale, Dorset caught a mild case of the Gilded Age bug as word about its beautiful surroundings and healing waters spread among the elite of the eastern cities.

Beyond Manchester, Route 7 begins a series of long stretches of open road between the intermittent principal towns of Rutland, Brandon, Middlebury, and finally Burlington that cover a distance of almost 100 miles.

The upper slopes of Stratton Mountain

The view from the 3875-ft. summit of Stratton Mountain extends enormous distances in every direction. On a clear day it is possible to see Mount Washington, New Hampshire, over 100 miles away. The peak of Mt. Equinox, in the Taconic Range to the west, is also visible, and, nearer by, neighboring ski area Bromley can be seen to the north.

The alpine village at the base of Stratton features this iconic clock tower.

Dorset marble quarry.

From Manchester you pass through East Dorset and just down the road from this hamlet you will encounter the diminutive Emerald Lake State Park which is a very attractive place to spend a peaceful respite from the road. The headwaters of Otter Creek, the other principal river along Route 7, and the longest river in Vermont, form near Emerald Lake. Otter Creek flows almost unnoticed alongside Route 7 until well beyond Wallingford.

Three more miles down the road the village of Danby is set just off the road. Like Dorset, Danby enjoyed its heyday when precious Danby marble was being quarried for distant projects. A large quantity of Danby marble was commissioned for the construction of Washington, D.C. Although production is well below its peak of the early 1900s, Danby marble has a world-class reputation and is widely sought-after.

The townspeople of Danby take great pride in the fact that Pearl S. Buck, the first woman to win both a Pulitzer and a Nobel Prize for literature, settled in Danby for the last few years of her life and, smitten by the town, gave generously to help restore some of their historic buildings. The serpentine drive up Brook Road to Danby Four Corners is beautiful. It leads to Tinmouth Road which runs parallel to Route 7 and can be used as an alternate route to Wallingford.

Wallingford is a pleasant small town on Otter Creek which is still little more than a brook at this point. The town centers on Route 7 and there are many well-kept Victorian homes, antique shops and small businesses that line the street. At the main intersection in town, where Route 7 crosses Route 140, there is a small library and a striking three-story Italianate building that looks as if it dropped out of the sky from somewhere along the Amalfi coast of Italy. The notable Old Stone Shop, located just south of the intersection, is famous for being the original home of America's oldest pitchfork manufacturer. Paul P. Harris, who was brought to Wallingford to live with his grandparents when he was three, founded The Rotary Club here.

Emerald Lake State Park.

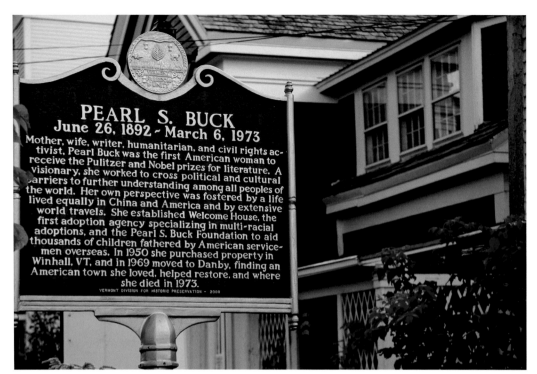

The village of Danby.

The "Old Stone Shop" building in Wallingford.

Downtown Wallingford along Route 7.

Wallingford to Middlebury

There is a pass through the Green Mountain chain to the east so the area around Wallingford and up into Rutland takes on a more gently rolling appearance. There are a number of local attractions including nearby Clarendon Gorge.

Rutland is the next major town along Route 7 and is actually the third largest city in Vermont. Unfortunately the Route 7 approach into and through Rutland is entirely commercial, but this belies the fact that it has a pleasant central area with several colonial churches.

The history of the greater Rutland area, that includes West Rutland and Proctor, is laced with controversy and political intrigue that actually left Rutland in the lurch at the peak of the marble industry's boom times. Through a series of deft, but highly controversial, business and political maneuvers over a period of 20 years, Redfield Proctor managed to consolidate an industry and tear apart a town all in the name of amassing an enormous personal fortune and having a town named after himself for good measure. The family's dual empires in state politics and the hugely influential marble industry thrived for over 50 years. Undoubtedly the most appealing legacy to this story is the elegant Marble Arch Bridge that spans Otter Creek in Proctor near the "The Great Falls."

Today Rutland continues to be an important crossroads for tourism and commerce, as its other principal road, Route 4, handles large a volume of traffic between central New England and the Adirondack region in New York. The bustling downtown area features a patchwork of attractive multi-story brick, turn-of-the-century buildings and the recently restored Paramount Theatre. The neo-classical theatre has been in operation since 1914 and was fully restored between 1997 and 2000 at the cost of $4 million. It is one of the few remaining Victorian opera houses in the entire country.

The small village of Pittsford, with its picturesque surroundings, lies between Rutland and Brandon.

Architecture along Merchants Row in downtown Rutland.

Opposite page
View of Rutland at dawn taken from the shoulder of Route 4 west of the city.

Rutland dressed up for the winter season.

The First Baptist Church and the Rutland County Courthouse on Center Street in downtown Rutland.

174

Architectural detail on Merchants Row.

175

The center of Rutland on Route 7.

The Proctor Marble Arch bridge is one of the reminders of the heady days of the second half of the 19th century when the railroads finally reached the Rutland area and the marble industry expanded rapidly.

I found this barn on one of the back roads of East Pittsford.

Countryside west of Pittsford just off of Route 7

177

Brandon is the next of what I call the historic marble towns along the way. To its benefit, Brandon was just far enough north of Rutland that it was spared the ugly politics of Rutland and Proctor and it has a genuinely friendly demeanor.

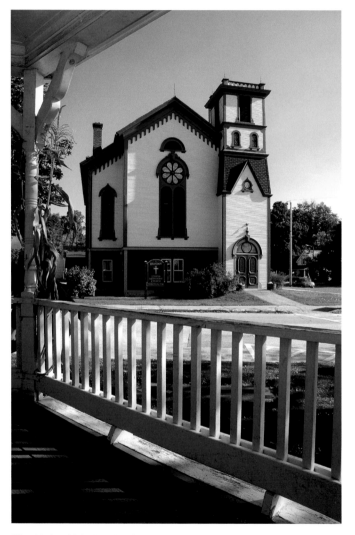

The United Methodist Church viewed from the bandstand on the village green in Brandon.

The Cooley Bridge in Pittsford is a 50-foot town lattice structure dating to 1849.

The village green in Brandon.

View from the shoulder of Route 7 north of Brandon.

The Civil War Monument in Brandon.

Route 7 continues through scenic rolling countryside on the run up to Middlebury. A few miles south of Middlebury you can visit Lake Dunsmore just off to the east of the neighboring towns of Leicester and Salisbury. There is also beautiful countryside to the west on Route 73 that leads to Sudbury and Orwell.

The picturesque hamlet of Orwell is situated about eight miles west of Brandon on Route 73 and makes for another pleasant side trip off of Route 7.

Lake Dunsmore has Hogback Mountain as its backdrop. This is different from the small Hogback Range that can be seen from Mt. Philo further north.

The iconic Congregational Church on the village green in Middlebury.

Opposite page
Scenery seen from the shoulder
of Route 7 in Salisbury.

More than you might think, Middlebury is profoundly linked to much of the revolutionary and cultural spirit of America. For example, early in its history Middlebury's population suffered egregiously when the town was sacked and burned during Carleton's Raid in October, 1778. John Deere, inventor of the steel plow that made the mass cultivation of the American plains possible, was born in Rutland. In 1821, at the age 17, he moved to Middlebury to apprentice in a blacksmith's shop. He spent four years in Middlebury learning the skills that paved the way to his invention. And, as discussed earlier, Robert Frost's long association with Middlebury and Bread Loaf made the town a world-renowned breeding ground for great literature.

Middlebury College is one of Americas finest small liberal arts schools and, along with Williams College to the south, is among a handful that are known as the "Little Ivy Schools." Like Williams, the college's campus boasts a Performing Arts Center and a well-regarded Museum of Fine Art. The town itself is an impeccably maintained oasis of beautiful historic hotels and inns, lively boutiques, and, of course, an obligatory steepled colonial church.

Middlebury College campus.

What would Vermont be without pure maple syrup?

The steeple of the Congregational Church rises above the trees on the village green in downtown Middlebury.

The general store in Ripton.

Above and opposite: The beautiful and distinct architecture of the campus at Bread Loaf is set against the even more impressive landscape of the Green Mountain National Forest. On the way here from Ripton you pass the Robert Frost Interpretive Trail and just two miles beyond here is Middlebury Gap and Middlebury College Snow Bowl.

Middlebury to Ferrisburgh

Sunrise over the Green Mountains and Route 7 in New Haven.

View from the shoulder of
Route7 in New Haven.

189

The view east to the Green Mountains from the shoulder of Route 7 in New Haven.

As Route 7 heads north out of Middlebury, it continues its gradual disengagement from the mountains to the east and the landscape opens to a wide, mostly flat plain. Vergennes is the next stop and there are no villages in between.

Vergennes has many unusual distinctions. It is actually officially classified as a city, which makes it the smallest city by population not only in Vermont, but in all of America. Furthermore, it is the oldest city in the state.

Vergennes was incorporated as a city in 1788 because it was felt at the time that its optimal location at a point of rapidly running water on Otter Creek would stimulate the growth of a diverse portfolio of industries. It worked for a time, but the decline of the shipping industry and the inability to create railroad access handicapped the city's growth. Today there are only 2,800 inhabitants of Vergennes.

It is not clear from where, or who, the city's French name is derived, but it is a noticeable juxtaposition to the purely British place names of almost every other town and city along Route 7. Vergennes's 1897 Opera House was completely restored and reopened as a movie house and performing arts space in 1997 as part of a long-term revitalization plan to focus on tourism and entertainment. The Opera House has a storied history that includes a visit by President William Howard Taft who spoke at a ceremony celebrating the 300th anniversary of "the discovery" of Lake Champlain.[23] Vergennes was also an important strategic naval base during the War of 1812.

There is a beautiful view of Vergennes from the roadside Prospect Cemetery which is perched on a hill above the power station on Otter Creek.

The Otter Creek falls complex viewed from the Vergennes Falls Park at the end of Mechanic Street. The two buildings in the middle of the photograph are the town water works and a former grist mill.

Downtown Vergennes has numerous shops and restaurants with seating areas raised above the sidewalk. The streets around the city green, also known as City Park, are colorfully decorated with hanging flower baskets and banners.

The view from the balcony of the Franklin House building on Main Street at dusk.

The 1897 Opera House has been the centerpiece of a city revitalization plan to draw tourism to Vergennes. The building has been completely restored and houses the Town Hall on the first floor and the theatre above.

From Vergennes, Route 7 skirts along the Lake Champlain shoreline for the last twenty miles into Burlington, providing occasional glimpses of the lake. Not far up the road from Vergennes is Rokeby Museum, the converted brick house of the family of Rowland E. Robinson. The home is one of the many along Route 7 that served as safe houses on the Underground Railroad.

When it comes to capturing Americana, road signs can make excellent subject matter. In rural Vermont, where billboards are practically non-existent there are many examples of creative signage like this one in Ferrisburgh

This dilapidated historic round barn is located just off Route 7 across from the entrance to Rokeby Museum. Chances are it will be gone in just a few more years.

Roadside field in Ferrisburgh.

Coleman Corner is nothing more than a cluster of buildings on the high banks above Lewis Creek on Old Hollow Road, but being a Midwesterner I couldn't help noticing this scene and wanting to capture it. I was drawn to the road because of its name and wound up enjoying the network of hilly back roads it led me to in Monkton, Charlotte, and Hinesburg.

Ferrisburgh to Burlington

196

This series of photographs was taken from just before the sun cleared the peaks of the Green Mountains until about an hour after sunset. A storm had come across the Adirondacks the night before leaving a fresh blanket of snow on the mountain peaks across the lake. In this frame, looking toward Split Rock mountain and Bart Royce Hill on the New York shore, you can see the red glow of the sun's first rays bouncing off the taller inland peaks. The second frame, the cover photograph for this book, is the view due south from Mt. Philo. The faint grey line of Route 7 can be seen in the large shadow just to the right of the center of the picture and Snake Mountain is the prominent peak on the horizon. The third shot shows the view to the southeast over Monkton, Starksboro, and Bristol. Mt. Fuller is in the foreground and beyond it are the Hogback Mountains and the distant peaks of Mt. Abraham, Prospect Rock, and Mt. Grant. The last photograph shows a view similar to this one across Lake Champlain with the foreground plains now bathed in warm early morning light.

The view from Mt. Philo State Park can be beautiful on any given day, but in one gorgeous sunrise I was treated to a one-and-a-half hour display of light and color that I will always remember. The 270-degree range of views from a series of points along an exposed rock ledge allows the visitor to get a sense of the grandeur of the entire Lake Champlain region as it spans across two large mountain ranges.

The turn-off for Mt. Philo is about seven miles north of Vergennes on the right side as you travel north. Although the mountain outcropping is only 968 feet high, it is so isolated on the plain that the unobstructed views seem to go on forever and make you feel as though you are several hundred, if not a thousand, feet higher. The park is a popular hiking destination for locals and visitors alike and weekends can become very crowded. Weddings and special events are also popular at the summit where there is a rustic cabin.

This photograph, while very similar to the second one in the previous series, was taken with a telephoto lens so the trail of Route 7 is more clearly visible running up through the center of the frame.

The countryside in the four townships that surround Mt. Philo is a beautiful expanse of rolling hills, small mountains, and fetching sections of shoreline. To the west, around the back of Mt. Philo and a mile-or-two away down dirt side roads, are two covered bridges over Lewis Creek, and a fishing pond is not far away in Monkton Ridge.

Sequin Bridge in Charlotte.

Lake Champlain, Shelburne; with a coffee by your side and a cell tower nearby there couldn't be a better internet café anywhere in the world.

Although there are beautiful pastoral farming scenes all around, there are some where all the elements come together perfectly, at the right time of day so that the resulting photograph has much more than that just-another-cliché-barn-shot look.

Lake Champlain at dusk looking southwest toward Split Rock Point in New York.

Not surprisingly, both the region around Burlington and the city itself offer an abundance of things to see and do. Indeed, for a city of only 40,000 or so, Burlington has a amazing number and range of attractions. As you approach Burlington from Charlotte, whose tiny, endearing town center is a few hundred yards west of Route 7 along Ferry Road, you soon begin to get a taste of what there is to do here. Shelburne is the polished exurb of Burlington that you roll into after passing the popular Vermont Teddy Bear Company factory. Shelburne was chartered in 1763 by the aforementioned Benning Wentworth under the same New Hampshire Grant that seems to have pertained to half the state. The name of Shelburne is derived from a prominent Britishman of the day, the noble Member of Parliament William Fitz-morris Petty, Second Earl of Shelburne. As was common in the day, a not-so-minor clerical error was made in the drafting of the appropriate paperwork that established the boundaries of the town, summarily resulting in the elimination of fourteen square miles of land from the town's tax base.[24]

During the town's first fifty years, development followed the established continuum for small central and northern Vermont towns and villages: gristmills, sawmills, and fulling mills were built to support the agricultural activities and some light industrial enterprises existed. The conclusion of the War of 1812, however, ushered in a vibrant period based on lake commerce and shipbuilding.

Iconic scenery from the shoulder of Route 7 in Charlotte.

The shipyard in Shelburne Harbor pumped out elegant steamships that plied the lake as both freight and passenger boats. One of the finest examples, *The Ticonderoga*, has been preserved in dry dock as the centerpiece of the unique outdoor museum of history in Shelburne. Indeed, many artifacts of New England frontier life, both large and small, can be enjoyed at the museum.

The *Ticonderoga* at Shelburne Farms. You can step aboard and witness the grandeur of this beautiful ship;

The commercial area of Shelburne occupies both sides of a half-mile stretch of Route 7 leading up to the town's principal intersection. There is an obligatory panoply of tourist shops as well as some fine restaurants, several inns, and a very friendly independent book store. The shoreline area west of Shelburne village has a maze of narrow country roads, all of which, it seems, eventually lead to Shelburne Farms. This isn't such a bad thing since Shelburne Farms is a grand complex of environmentally friendly agricultural operations under the auspices of a non-profit organization that has maintained the vision of its original owner.

The railroad baron Dr. William Stewart Webb and his wife, Lila Vanderbilt, commissioned the Gilded Age summer home in the late 1880s with the intent of not only having a palatial summer retreat but also creating a model sustainable agricultural enterprise. For about 20-25 years they succeeded, but eventually it began to sag under the weight of its financial requirements. In 1972 descendents of the Webbs turned the 3,800 acre property over to the non-profit that has maintained control of it ever since. The 25-bedroom waterfront mansion is now an exclusive hotel and the farm operations continue to develop innovative farming techniques and promote educational programs.

The coach barn at Shelburne Farms.

The horse breeding barn at Shelburne Farms.

The other sprawling public attraction in Shelburne is the aforementioned Shelburne Museum which is similar to Henry Ford's visionary Greenfield Village in Dearborn, Michigan. This outstanding collection of iconic symbols of the first 200 years of New England life, from a stone cottage to a one-room school house to an apothecary shop, allows one to step back in time in an almost utopian interactive environment.

The unusual horseshoe barn at Shelburne Museum was built on site in 1949.

The round barn at Shelburne Museum was relocated from East Passumpsic, Vermont, and dates to 1901.

Going north, Shelburne gives way to South Burlington, where Route 7 becomes a three-mile stretch of modern office buildings, shiny car dealerships, and chain establishments of all kinds until you enter the original residential suburbs of Burlington. With just 40,000 inhabitants Burlington is by far the smallest principal city of any state in the coun-try, but it benefits from this fact far more than it suffers any detriment. Burlington is a manageable, fun, and eminently friendly city that seems to have only one major drawback—really long winters. But for visitors who are accustomed to exercising reasonable discretion about where they go and when they go there, this too can be overcome.

The shoreline of Lake Champlain between Shelburne Farms and Shelburne Village.

Burlington, also known as Vermont's Queen City, experienced its rise in the 1820s and 1830s when three crucial canals, the Erie, Champlain, and Chambly, were built, opening uninterrupted shipping lanes to New York City and the St. Lawrence Seaway. The prosperous times endured until the conclusion of World War II, after which the city suffered several decades of either stagnation or decline. Like many of the communities in the Route 7 corridor, the last 25 years have been a period of introspection and recovery for this great city. A once dead and decaying waterfront has been transformed with parks and bicycle rail trails, and the downtown area has been spruced up with a fashionable pedestrian mall.

Scenes from Waterfront Park, Burlington.

Church Street, Burlington.

Citizens of Burlington have retained a connection to, and involvement with, their inner city and, to a certain extent, shunned the mall-and-suburb mentality that has afflicted many other cities. The downtown parks are safe and vibrant and there is usually considerable foot traffic on the streets at night around City Hall Park and the Church Street Mall. In season, a weekend market occupies City Hall Park and attracts large crowds.

The scale of the architecture has also been well managed so that there is plentiful sunlight and a sense of openness. Burlington's image got a welcome boost in the 1980s with the founding of Ben & Jerry's Ice Cream, and several other progressive companies, like Burton, of snowboarding fame, now have extensive operations here.

City Hall Park, Burlington.

Typical late-1800s architecture in downtown Burlington along College Street.

Cityscape of Burlington taken from the Waterfront.

Of course a large measure of the atmosphere of the city is attributable to the presence of the neighboring University of Vermont and Champlain College which are located blocks from the city center. They also contribute significantly to the demand for diverse cultural events that are supported by venues like the Flynn Center for the Performing Arts, a restored vaudeville playhouse similar to the Mahaiwe Theatre, 220 miles south in Great Barrington. Finally, the ECHO Lake Aquarium and Science Center is the centerpiece of Waterfront Park where the Spirit of Ethan Allen cruise ship operates lake tours and hosts floating special events.

Williams Hall is one of the historic landmark buildings on University of Vermont's University Row. The University was chartered in 1791, and one of its founders was Ira Allen, brother of Route 7 namesake Ethan Allen.

The campus Green along University Row at the University of Vermont.

213

Burlington to Highgate Springs

At the north end of the city, just beyond North Beach Park, is the Ethan Allen Homestead. This is where the namesake of Route 7 retired to in 1784 until his death five years later.

Traveling north out of Burlington, there are three ways to cover the final fifty-odd miles to the Canadian border in Highgate Springs. One is the forbidden freeway method on Interstate 89. The other two, of course, involve the Ethan Allen Highway. About five miles north of Burlington, Route 2 shoots off from Route 7 veering in the direction of Grand Isle which is well worth a visit if for no other reason than the sense of release you can get from being on this completely unpretentious piece of the planet. Gone are almost all of the trappings of our material-obsessed world; this is just a pleasant stretch of road that connects a series of humble, but very worthy, towns. Fittingly, probably the foremost landmark on the Island is the Hyde Log Cabin, which is believed to be the oldest log cabin in the United States. There are also several sublime state parks spread along the Lake Champlain shores, and the occasional quirky icon to catch your eye. Route 2 crosses over to the Alburg Tongue from North Hero and from there you have, yet again, two choices for making the final push to Canada. Taking Route 78 just after Alburg Center returns you to Route 7 in Swanton.

The interior of Ethan Allen's modest frontier homestead above the Winooski River north of downtown Burlington.

The Hyde Log Cabin in South Hero on Grand Isle.

This is an example of a scene I saw that I thought was curious, charming, and playful at the same time. I don't recall ever having seen a penny-farthing tricycle before, and the juxtaposition of it appearing with a large barn that I was able to make appear small in the background was just something I wanted to share. I know that it's not the most technically amazing photograph I have ever taken, but I like it.

Surprisingly, the Grand Isle Lake House was not built as a Gilded Age mansion yet it functioned as a symbol of that era. Constructed by the Briggs family of Burlington in 1903 to serve as a hotel, it was originally named the Island Villa Hotel and drew wealthy patrons from Burlington and beyond.

The austere St. Joseph church in South Hero has the kind of American Gothic feel to it that defines Grand Isle.

215

Above and opposite page
Sunrise over the beautiful landscape in Fairfax, just east of Route 7.

If you stay on Route 7, or come back to it from Grand Isle, you will travel another five miles through the center of Milton and eventually come across Route 104A on the right side of the road. 104A, it turns out, leads no more than three or four miles out past Arrowhead Lake and along the Lemoille River to the pastoral countryside of Fairfax. It is a short detour that can be continued by taking 104 north to St. Albans where you can rejoin the Ethan Allen Highway thereby avoiding a somewhat blah stretch of it.

Lemoille River in East Georgia along 104A.

Remaining on Route 7 north of Milton, you pass by Hubbard Center and Georgia Center before reaching St. Albans. As was discussed in the earlier chapter about historical events that took place on or along Route 7, St. Albans was the scene of the infamous St. Albans Raid in 1864, which was an armed assault on the town by twenty-two rogue, and presumably lost and unsupervised, Confederate soldiers who created havoc while robbing three banks, stealing horses, and firing indiscriminately at whatever moved.

The town has a beautiful central park with footpaths and an ornate green, tiered fountain that is surrounded by trademark late-1800s New England brick commercial buildings. St. Albans has a Mayberry, U.S.A., atmosphere and has been making earnest efforts in recent years to boost civic pride and stimulate positive growth. To the west a mile or two is the sister community, St. Albans Bay, which has several shops and a wooded lake front recreational park. Each year St. Albans hosts the Vermont Maple Festival, which has earned it the title Maple Sugar Capital of the World.

The last town of any size along Route 7 before reaching the northern state border is Swanton. Like St. Albans, Swanton is an extremely welcoming community with rich historical ties to the region. The last settlement of any kind along Route 7 is Highgate Springs. Two miles beyond the small town center Route 7 comes to an abrupt and unceremonious end at a guardrail that blocks access to the customs plaza whose only approach today is by way of I-89.

Hopefully now you will agree, if you didn't already, that Route 7, the Ethan Allen Highway, is one of America's great roads and is deserving of at least one pilgrimage, or even a partial one, at some point in your lifetime.

There are countless local historical societies sprinkled along Route 7, often right on the road, and there is something profoundly endearing about the fact that they are there at all. No matter how humble or unassuming, they are symbols of the essential enduring civic pride that many Americans share and cherish. And very often they are well worth visiting for even a few minutes.

The lovely fountain, that could have been plucked from a Parisian plaza, graces the north end of Taylor Park in St. Albans.

Solid brick churches and the St. Albans Historical Museum line the east side of the village green raised up slightly over a row of commercial buildings on the opposite side of the park.

Hudak Farm on Route 7 in Swanton is an unusual building that immediately caught my eye. Marie and Richard Hudak are the owners. Richard hails form eastern Europe and built the main building in the traditional wooden tracery style that can be seen throughout eastern Europe and Russia.

The Hudak Farm.

Highgate Springs.

222

Bibliography

Boughton, Mark D., Mayor. "2006-2007 Adopted Budget, City of Danbury, Connecticut" 2006.

Hagstrom Map Company. *Fairfield County.* Long Island City, New York: Langenscheidt Publishing Group, 2001

Owens, Carole. "Father of the shock absorber." *The Berkshire Eagle,* July 28, 2008

Room, Adrian. *Placenames of the World.* Jefferson, North Carolina: McFarland, 2003

Secker-Walker, Joyce, Ethan Allen: Highlights in the Life of Vermont's Folk Hero. Burlington, Vermont: Ethan Allen homestead Trust, 1993

Vergennes, The City of. *The Vermont Guidebook: Touring Vermont's Oldest City.* Lake Champlain Basin Program, www.vergennes.org (accessed November 29, 2008)

Washington, Ida H., and Paul A. Washington. *Carleton's Raid.* Weybridge, Vermont: Cherry Tree Books, 1998

Websites
www.cttrust.org (accessed 12/06/08)
www.duboisic.org (accessed 1/17/09)
www.gbcnet.com (accessed 11/28/08)
www.normanrockwell.com (accessed 01/22/09)
www.norwalk.ws (accessed 12/12/08)
www.pittsfield-ma.org (accessed 12/09/08 & 01/22/09)
www.rowaytonhistoricalsociety.org (accessed 01/17/09)
www.s230494718.online.us (accessed 12/10/08)
www.tfhrc.gov (accessed 12/12/08)
www.townoflenox.com (accessed 1/9/09)
www.trafficsign.us (accessed 11/28/08)
www.us-highways.com (accessed 01/17/09)
www.us-highways.com (accessed 11/12/08)
www.wikipedia.org (accessed 11/15/08)

The *Spirit of Ethan Allen* is the largest cruise ship on Lake Champlain.

Endnotes

[1]"Current Comment" *The Hartford Courant,* August 12, 1932 (Courtesy of the Connecticut Historical Society)

[2]U.S. Highways From US 1 to (US 830). www.us-highways.com/#uslog (accessed 1/17/09)

[3]"Fort Ethan Allen Highway Completed," *The Hartford Courant,* Sept. 22, 1930 (Courtesy of the Connecticut Historical Society)

[4]*Ibid*

[5]"Three Connecticut Highways Which Legislators Propose To Name After Historical Figures," *The Hartford Courant,* February 19, 1933 (Courtesy of the Connecticut Historical Society)

[6]"Current Comment" *op. cit.*

[7]"Three Connecticut Highways…" *op. cit.*

[8]"Ethan Allen Highway Objective of Auto Club Tour" *The Hartford Courant,* October 2, 1932 (Courtesy of the Connecticut Historical Society)

[9] Jocelyn Secker-Walker, *Ethan Allen: Highlights in the Life of Vermont's Folk Hero,* Burlington, Vermont: Ethan Allen Homestead Trust, 1993, p. 2, 6-7

[10]www.pittsfield-ma.org/subpage.asp?ID=226

[11]www.duboislc.org/html/DuBoisBio.html

[12]www.lookingforadventure.com/historyofdanbury.html

[13]Adrian Room, *Placenames of the World,* Jefferson, North Carolina: McFarland, 2003, p. 99

[14] Mark D. Boughton, Mayor, "2006-2007 Adopted Budget, City of Danbury, Connecticut" 2006, www.ci.danbury.ct.us/filestorage/41/180/12737/5205/06-07CoverPages.pdf

[15]www.cttrust.org/index.cgi/2016

[16]*Ibid.*

[17]Hagstrom Map Company, Fairfield County, Long Island City, New York: Langenscheidt Publishing Group, 2001, p. 75

[18]www.townoflenox.com/Public_Documents/LenoxMA_WebDocs/about

[19]*Ibid*

[20]www.pittsfield-ma.org/history.asp

[21]Carole Owens, "Father of the shock absorber," *The Berkshire Eagle* 28 July, 2008

[22]www.s230494718.onlinehome.us, Town of Williamstown, Massachusetts 01267, page: History of Williamstown.

23   The City of Vergennes. *The Vermont Guidebook: Touring Vermont's Oldest City.* Lake Champlain Basin Program.

24   www.virtualvermont.com/towns/shelburne.html#about

Howden Farm, Ashley Falls, Massachusetts.